FREEDOM'S SHORE

RUSSELL DUNCAN

FREEDOM'S SHORE

Tunis Campbell
and the Georgia Freedmen

THE UNIVERSITY OF GEORGIA PRESS

ATHENS AND LONDON

© 1986 by the University of Georgia Press
Athens, Georgia 30602
All rights reserved

Designed by Kathi L. Dailey
Set in 10 on 13 Century Schoolbook
with Clarendon display

The illustration on the title page is a drawing of Tunis
Gulic Campbell, from his 1848 book (Moorland-Spingarn
Research Center, Howard University).

The paper in this book meets the guidelines for
permanence and durability of the Committee on
Production Guidelines for Book Longevity of the
Council on Library Resources.

Printed in the United States of America

90 89 88 87 86   5 4 3 2 1

Library of Congress Cataloging in Publication Data

Duncan, Russell.
Freedom's shore.

Bibliography: p.
Includes index.
1. Campbell, Tunis.   2. Reconstruction—
Georgia.   3. Freedmen—Georgia.   4. Georgia—Race
relations.   5. Afro-Americans—Georgia—History—19th
century.   I. Title.
F291.C2D86   1986   975.8′00496073   86–6914
ISBN 0–8203–0876–5 (alk. paper)
ISBN 0–8203–0905–2 (pbk.: alk. paper)

To Joan, Betty, Pete, Mary Ella, and J.W.
FOR DEBTS I CAN NEVER REPAY

They bore me o'er the river, across to freedom's shore
    My senses they were reeling,
    Yet the truth it was revealing,
    Unto my wounded feeling;
That I was slave no more.

HENRY MCNEAL TURNER, 1874

CONTENTS

PREFACE

adical Reconstruction held out the promise of equality for all men and women. After a century of bondage, blacks rejoiced at the prospects of change which they saw all around them. In 1865 along the coast of Georgia, freedmen applied for and some got the forty acres of land that most expected to receive from the government. A few of the luckiest found mules to help them drag plows on the single-family or community farms that sprang up everywhere. Had the redistribution of land been more general and turned into lasting fact and not merely the short-lived aberration it proved to be, the revolutionary devices of the Emancipation Proclamation and the three postwar constitutional amendments might have moved America a long way toward realization of the American creed that all men are created equal.

This book presents an explanation of Tunis Campbell's tactics to change labor and social relationships in Georgia from ones of inequality to ones of equality. I have attempted to present Campbell as he was—an American who wanted to create a true color-blind democracy.

In 1874 another freedom fighter and friend of Campbell, Henry McNeal Turner, wrote a poem entitled "The Conflict for Civil Rights." The poem is unexceptional except as an optimistic appraisal that black folk will on one future day rise from society's depths to be admired everywhere. A line in Turner's poem provided this book's title: "They bore me o'er the river, across to freedom's shore." Of course, Turner meant the River Jordan and salvation from bondage, and that allusion itself would be sufficient. But the major setting of this book at the coast of Georgia during the first years after emancipation made the title even more appropriate. That Henry Turner shared Campbell's vision of equality, if not his methods, further convinced me. This book is about the struggle for human rights at freedom's shore.

MANY INDIVIDUALS have helped me in various ways. My debts to them are immense. I benefited greatly from their unselfish help.

Archivists and librarians not only found the items I requested but led me to other avenues and through other sources that have informed this work. I am indebted to nearly all the staff members of the University of Georgia library. They cheerfully ordered and reordered interlibrary resources, answered and reanswered questions, and voluntarily assisted my research well beyond the call of duty. I especially thank Larry Gulley, Robert M. Willingham, Jr., and Nelson Morgan for their expertise in rare books, maps, and manuscripts. Barbara Rystrom and Donna Dorsey deftly acquired materials from loaning libraries nationwide. Sarah Lockmiller's photographic talents produced "miracles" from old and battered materials.

At the Georgia Department of Archives and History, Virginia Shadron guided this greenhorn past unfathomable numbers of documents to those relevant to my topic. Gail Miller located many photographs found in this book. Gayle Peters, director of the Federal Archives in Atlanta, assisted me more than I had justifiable reason to expect. In Savannah, Barbara Bennett's unfailing expertise in the holdings of the Georgia Historical Society solved many dilemmas.

At the University of Georgia I shared companionship with many graduate students among whom I especially thank

Terri Blair, Winfield Myers, Michael Justus, and Tom Richey.

He said, "If you are not writing for publication, you are wasting your time." He raged, "Your prose simply must improve!" He suggested the topic and stood by ready to counsel. Unrelenting in demands for achievement yet patient in criticism and steadfast in guidance, Emory Thomas provided the confidence and contagious enthusiasm that sustained my efforts during the year of research and writing. I am grateful to him for his model as a scholar and a man.

Others improved the manuscript through careful, critical readings. I want to thank especially Numan V. Bartley and Charles E. Wynes for their help in shaping this work in its earliest stages. William M. Leary's support and suggestions convinced me and others that the thesis would be a book; he proved to be an indispensable link in the process. William S. McFeely's thorough critique led me to rethink and rewrite many pages. For the trouble he caused me and the warmth he extended, I offer my appreciation. Frank Saunders, C. Peter Ripley, and Larry Powell extended perspicacious commentary and suggestions that forced me to delete a few of my most outrageous passages.

Lester Stephens and Alf Heggoy graciously provided encouragement and support in the final stages of preparation. Nancy Heaton exhibited courage and skill by volunteering to type my scribbles. The University of Georgia's Office of the Vice President for Research contributed financial aid for this project.

During the course of this study many southerners opened their houses and hearts to me. I could not possibly thank them all here. Special thanks to Royce Hayes, superintendent of St. Catherines Island, and Betsy Hayes for allowing me to visit their island. I also must thank Bill Haynes, George Rogers, Mr. and Mrs. R. E. Gill, Bill and Barry Rosier, Virginia Steele Wood, and Kenneth H. Thomas.

Everyone associated with the University of Georgia Press extended patience, generous help, and the necessary editorial skill to bring this book into being, Editor Malcolm Call supported the manuscript from the beginning. Karen Orchard and Ellen Harris never failed to lift my spirits or offer timely suggestions. Kathi Dailey designed the visual and layout format. Trudie Calvert performed the yeoman's task of copyediting. Her eye for detail and uncanny ability to transform garbled ideas into understandable prose brought the manuscript into its final form.

My family never failed to give more than they got in return. They were always there to help me along. I have dedicated this book to those who dedicated so much to me.

Finally, Holly McCurry Duncan and Bonnie Katherine Duncan helped me keep what humanity I have. They decreased all the pressures I put on myself by always being ready if I needed smiles and hugs. I often needed both.

Coastal Georgia, circa 1870. Drawn by the Cartographic Services
Laboratory, University of Georgia.

worked to implement free-labor plantations. Others, many of whom had waged a lifelong struggle to abolish slavery, came south to further the revolution by helping the former slaves toward free-in-fact equality. Several hundreds of these idealists, who held the freedmen's advancement higher than personal gains, were white; a few hundred were black.[11]

These northern black idealists, trained in leadership by their previous participation in the abolitionist movement or as ministers of the gospel or as teachers, found the masses of aspiring, unsophisticated freedmen in need of leaders. They united with talented native blacks who, for the most part, had been free before the war or had held relatively advantaged positions as slaves. Many black leaders turned naturally to politics to help advance the freedmen. In every case, as a recent study of black leaders in the Reconstruction era found, these black politicians gained office from a base in the black community.[12]

In every southern state a few blacks, whether free or slave in origin, stood up to lead the freedmen and drew what power they achieved from strong black constituencies. In Alabama James T. Rapier, a free-born black from Florence with a Canadian education, built a powerful political organization and spent his life trying to improve his race. Hiram R. Revels and Blanche K. Bruce represented Mississippi in the U.S. Senate. Revels, America's first black senator, had been born free in North Carolina, educated in Illinois, ordained a minister in the African Methodist Episcopal church, and enlisted in a black regiment that served in Mississippi during the war. Bruce was a former Virginia slave who escaped to Missouri on the eve of the Civil War, studied at Oberlin College, and moved to Mississippi in 1869. Bruce, Revels, and Rapier enjoyed more than a modicum of white support, and favored moderate goals. Revels even played a dubious role in returning Democrats to power.[13]

Josiah Walls, born a slave in 1842 in Virginia, escaped

INTRODUCTION

Emancipation is one fact, and effective liberty is another. Man does not have all his rights and privileges,
he does not have free exercise of his faculties and skills
by simple consequence of the abolition of slavery. Old
attitudes survive the proclamation of liberty, and old
interests persist through the changes brought about
by a new regime. After slavery has disappeared from
the law, the former rulers seem to want to preserve
slavery in fact.

LA TRIBUNE DE LA NOUVELLE ORLEANS, 1865

The war ended, but the revolution continued. Nothing in nineteenth-century America approached
the radicalism of the effort to transform freedmen into free men. The attempt to raise instantly
a class and create a color-blind democracy involved the up-
heaval of long-established norms. Although the issue of
slavery had been settled forever by the blood of more than
half a million Americans, emancipation raised many new
questions: What policy should be taken toward the former
slaves? How would the blacks handle their new freedom?
Could the revolution lift them into the American mainstream? Everywhere these questions demanded answers,
but nowhere more than in the South's "Empire" state.[1]

In Georgia, 462,198 former slaves shook themselves in the
new light of freedom. But exactly what did freedom mean?
Few blacks had land or money or property, and few whites

had the inclination to give them any. Some freedmen remained on plantations and worked for former masters or neighboring whites. Others fled to cities to search for jobs away from the scene of their former bondage. Some roved the countryside looking for relatives or the promise at the end of freedom's rainbow. Many simply waited and watched, hoping to make sense of the confusion of their new status.

The war destroyed the fortunes of many whites; the loss in slaves alone in Georgia reached nearly $500 million. Additionally, whites experienced the ultimate sacrifice as sons, fathers and brothers did not come home or came home maimed. Among Georgia communities McIntosh County provides a lucid example. Three hundred of that coastal Georgia county's sons marched off to war; fifty returned. Many of the survivors had been crippled, blinded, or mentally wounded by bullets, dysentery, or pneumonia, or by a hundred other accidents of fate.[2]

McIntosh County, in 1860, was at the geographic center of the state's rice coast, bounded on the south by Glynn and Wayne counties, on the north by Liberty County, and on the east by the Atlantic Ocean. A string of richly fertile, heavily timbered barrier islands protected the mainland and provided the lowlands required to grow rice. The Altamaha River, one of Georgia's principal arteries, rose in the piedmont, where its two main tributaries, the Ocmulgee and the Oconee, flowed southward, paralleling each other past Atlanta and Athens through the fall line cities of Macon and Milledgeville before converging near Hazelhurst and reaching the sea below Darien, some 250 miles downstream. The Altamaha brought fresh water to the coast and interplayed with powerful tides to provide planters with a natural hydraulic system by which to flood and drain their rice fields.[3]

Because of the river, which made up for the lack of rail transportation or an adequate interconnecting road system, the county seat of Darien prospered. Darien's deepwater port provided a suitable harbor for merchant and timber ships from industrial nations that bought the cotton, white pine, cypress, and rice that accumulated on the docks. Upriver cotton growers floated "Oconee boxes"—rafts constructed of large logs, roughly hewn, and piled with bagged cotton as high as fourteen feet—from the central Georgia black belt to the coastal shippers. When the "boxes" reached Darien, men removed the cotton to waiting ships, then broke apart the rafts and sold the timber to be cut or resold by one of the local sawmills. In 1835 nearly 130,000 bales arrived in Darien by raft. By 1840 at least twelve steamboats plied the river hauling cotton between Macon and Darien. In addition to the short-staple cotton of middle Georgia, merchantmen loaded their holds with Sea Island cotton, desired by northern and European mills for its long fibers and luxuriant texture.[4]

One of Georgia's oldest cities, Darien grew up on the site of Fort King George, a military outpost erected in 1721 to protect England's territorial claims against Spanish incursions. Scottish immigrants founded New Inverness in 1736, three years after James Oglethorpe established Savannah and the colony of Georgia, but later they changed the name to Darien in memory of the ill-fated group of Highlanders who had attempted a settlement on the Isthmus of Panama in 1697. In its earliest years, Darien distinguished itself primarily by an antislavery petition in 1739. Countering a request Savannah colonists sent to the Trustees asking permission to import and enslave Africans, the Darienites anxiously prophesied: "It is shocking to human nature that any race of mankind and their Posterity, should be sentenced to perpetual slavery, nor in justice can we think otherwise of it, than that they are thrown amongst us to be our Scourge one day or another for our Sins: and as Freedome to them must be as dear to us, what a scene of Horrour must it

bring about!" Despite this noble sentiment, when the Trustees approved slaveholding for Georgians and overthrew the
restriction limiting the size of land grants, the promise of
substantial material gains quickly brought slaves to Darien.
Gangs of chattels made it possible and profitable to grow
rice on a large scale along the tidal rivers near the coast.[5]

By 1790 a few planters had established small cotton- and
rice-growing operations there. Around 1800 Jacob Waldburg
and Thomas Spalding separately bought two of the largest
barrier islands, St. Catherines in Liberty County and Sapelo
in McIntosh County, and developed them into enormously
lucrative enterprises. Spalding introduced the Sea Island
cotton to the area and preached a "gospel of grass," promoting the planting of rice, cotton, wheat, and sugarcane. By
1860 Waldburg operated two large plantations on St. Catherines and owned many other properties in Savannah,
where he maintained a large "city house." He worked 255
slaves on land valued at $193,000. In 1853 Spalding died,
but his heirs continued working the nearly 300 Sapelo
slaves.[6]

By 1830 rice surpassed cotton as "king" in coastal counties. Pierce Butler purchased an island just south of Darien
and just far enough from the coast for sufficient fresh water
to permit rice operations. By 1850 his heir, by the same
name, owned 524 slaves and was probably the richest
planter in the area. The latter Butler married English
actress and abolitionist Frances Anne Kemble. He brought
her to Georgia, from their Philadelphia residence, in the
winter of 1838. Fanny scrutinized southern life and listened
sympathetically to the bondsmen. She was horrified at the
dehumanizing effects of slavery and in her journal described
the "barbarous aristocracy" of rice planters. The rice opera-
tion succeeded, however; in 1845 alone slaves grew nearly
one million pounds of marketable rice for Butler.[7]

Others also prospered, and the rice aristocracy became

one of the wealthiest, most clannish cliques in the South. On the Altamaha River plantations where Butler's Island was located, 2,785 slaves worked 8,000 acres to reap more than 255,000 bushels of rice producing a net profit of $154,000 in 1859. The 1860 census shows that the 41,084 Georgia slaveholders had an average of 11.2 slaves each. Nearly doubling the state average, Liberty County's 277 slaveholding families (of a total of 460 families) owned 6,083 people, or 21.9 each. In McIntosh County, 155 of 301 families held 4,063 slaves, an average of 26.2, almost two and one-half times the state average. Historians generally agree that to own twenty or more slaves made one a "planter"; anyone owning fifty or more certainly ranked among the wealthiest 2 or 3 percent of all Americans. In 1860 no less than twenty-three McIntosh County planters owned more than fifty slaves; six more owned between forty and fifty. The largest slaveholders included Pierce Butler (505), Randolph Spalding (252), P. M. Nightingale (169), Jacob Barrett (155), Norman Gignilliat (152), M. I. Kenan (118), William R. Gignilliat (117), Charles H. Hopkins (106), R. L. Morris (98), William Cook (96), and W. H. Atwood (84). Not surprisingly, the prewar members of the state legislature represented a near roll call of slaveholding aristocrats. The rice aristocracy dominated the land and all who lived there.[8]

Whites not engaged in staple-crop agriculture worked as subsistence farmers, mechanics, merchants, clerks, timber workers, pilots, constables, lawyers, and at other occupations in town. Few whites lived outside the town of Darien, and the county's vast inland area of piney woods remained sparsely populated. Only the hardiest whites braved the McIntosh climate. The long, steamy summers coupled with the large marshy areas and the oft-flooded ricelands produced an ideal breeding ground for mosquitoes. Planters filled their journals and diaries with accounts of how many slaves got sick or died from the disease-carrying insects and

climate. If that were not enough, the gnats, sand fleas, rat-
tlesnakes, and alligators joined with an average rainfall of
forty-nine inches, heaviest in June through September, to
create an unfavorable environment.[9]

The wealthy planters usually spent only two or three
months a year in residence on the coast; most retreated to
more agreeable climates and grander settings in Savannah,
Charleston, or New York during the rest of the year. Those
of less affluence found some relief in their summer homes
on high ground four miles north of Darien at "The Ridge."
Others lived in Darien, tied there by mercantile interests or
the timber trade. Of course, having no choice, blacks worked
year-round in the malarial swamps. During the winter the
planters returned to look after their interests, mingle with
others of their class, enjoy a more temperate climate, and
admire the beauty of the land. The county was indeed beau-
tiful. Magnolia trees and hyacinth blooms dotted the mas-
sive lawns. Magnificent ancient oaks draped in Spanish
moss seemed to express the permanence and beauty of the
South.[10]

Today one can visit Thomas Spalding's Ashantilly, built
around 1800, still owned privately, and located two miles
north of Darien, to sense the grandeur enjoyed by the rice
aristocracy. Ashantilly evokes the romance of the past with
its striking architecture and size. The aged oak sentinels
covered with gray moss create a canopy over its enormous
lawn stretching into the distance to a bluff and the sea
marsh beyond. Ashantilly and its setting emphasize the reality behind the myth of the Old South.

Many southerners held the lifestyle of the aristocracy as
an ideal, proof that the southern ideology and way of life
offered the best of the American Dream. It did not matter
that few climbed the ladder to success; the example of the
great planters provided instant status to all white people.
Even the poorest and meanest of the poor whites accepted

the planters' ideology and their hegemony and knew they
shared privileges with an elite class. They could never sink
to the lowest level of society for black slaves occupied that
position.

The Civil War overturned the way of life and threatened
the ideology of the entire white South. The loss of sons, fathers, or brothers on far-off battlefields had been easier to
accept than what came next—the end of a way of life. The
revolution that freed the slaves now threatened to lift them
to equal status and opportunity with whites, who saw themselves not only as betters but as masters of an inferior race.
Whites could not justify in their own minds any equal status
for the freedmen for to do so would inflict on them an al-
batross of guilt and would negate the reasons for their sacri-
fice of blood in the war. They held the Lost Cause inviolate.
Even poor whites could not join with blacks in a natural
struggle to raise their economic position because of the concept of race.

If southern blacks were to gain any semblance of equality
and achieve a biracial society in the postwar South, they
would have to take the necessary steps themselves. The
United States government had proved an uncertain ally.
Blacks could not simply depend on Yankees to defend their
freedom, give them land, or protect their families from former masters. After all, the government had given them land
under the Confiscation Acts (1861, 1862), Sherman's Order
No. 15 (1865), and Freedmen's Bureau (1865), only to take it
away again when planters forced the issue. Yet if black and
white southerners were to rise above their former relationships, they needed help from northerners. And the
northerners who helped most were those who came south
and stayed.

Carpetbaggers flocked into the old Confederacy, and not a
few filled their pockets at the expense of southerners both
black and white. But many of the "new masters" honestly

worked to implement free-labor plantations. Others, many of whom had waged a lifelong struggle to abolish slavery, came south to further the revolution by helping the former slaves toward free-in-fact equality. Several hundreds of these idealists, who held the freedmen's advancement higher than personal gains, were white; a few hundred were black.[11]

These northern black idealists, trained in leadership by their previous participation in the abolitionist movement or as ministers of the gospel or as teachers, found the masses of aspiring, unsophisticated freedmen in need of leaders. They united with talented native blacks who, for the most part, had been free before the war or had held relatively advantaged positions as slaves. Many black leaders turned naturally to politics to help advance the freedmen. In every case, as a recent study of black leaders in the Reconstruction era found, these black politicians gained office from a base in the black community.[12]

In every southern state a few blacks, whether free or slave in origin, stood up to lead the freedmen and drew what power they achieved from strong black constituencies. In Alabama James T. Rapier, a free-born black from Florence with a Canadian education, built a powerful political organization and spent his life trying to improve his race. Hiram R. Revels and Blanche K. Bruce represented Mississippi in the U.S. Senate. Revels, America's first black senator, had been born free in North Carolina, educated in Illinois, ordained a minister in the African Methodist Episcopal church, and enlisted in a black regiment that served in Mississippi during the war. Bruce was a former Virginia slave who escaped to Missouri on the eve of the Civil War, studied at Oberlin College, and moved to Mississippi in 1869. Bruce, Revels, and Rapier enjoyed more than a modicum of white support, and favored moderate goals. Revels even played a dubious role in returning Democrats to power.[13]

Josiah Walls, born a slave in 1842 in Virginia, escaped

slavery, entered the Union army in 1863, and taught in a
Florida Freedmen's Bureau school in 1866 before becoming
involved in that state's Radical politics. In South Carolina,
Robert Smalls, a former slave, gained fame by commandeer-
ing the Confederate steamer *Planter* and sailing past Fort
Sumter to gain freedom in 1862. He combined popularity
with racial pride and positive actions to establish a political
machine in Beaufort County powerfully backed by a seven-
to-one black majority. He remained in the state legislature
and U.S. Congress from 1868 to 1886, undoubtedly one of
the most successful of Reconstruction's black politicians.[14]

Black leaders had influence in all the Reconstruction leg-
islatures but controlled none of them. Six of the fourteen
blacks elected to the United States House of Representatives came from South Carolina. No black attained guber-
natorial office, and only a few became lieutenant governors
or secretaries of state. Generally, whites occupied those
positions. Yet it should be underscored that those blacks who
gained office promoted equality and ably established what
barriers they could erect to forestall Democratic resurgence.

Ultimately, though, these black leaders failed to halt the
counterrevolution of planter power that reestablished itself
everywhere by 1877. In Georgia, Redeemers took full control of the state government by 1872 with the ascendancy of
Democrat James M. Smith to the governor's chair. Even earlier, Congress revoked Georgia's restoration to the Union because white legislators expelled all blacks from the state
government in 1868. Altogether, Georgia was reconstructed
three times—first in 1865, under moderate Andrew Johnson's presidential plan which restored lands to planters and
denied black franchisement; then in 1868, under congressional Reconstruction; and finally in 1870, after the reseat-
ing of expelled legislators and ratification of the Fifteenth
Amendment. At the state level, then, Radical Reconstruction lasted, at most, four years.

The revolutionary aspects of emancipation cannot be over-stated. Abolishing slavery and enfranchising blacks upset traditional political, economic, and social mores, destroyed a way of life, and threatened southern ideology. Conflict be-tween former masters and bondsmen was inevitable. Blacks survived only through the establishment of strong commu-nities and by the grace of time given them by Radical leaders.

In McIntosh County, a black radical, Tunis Campbell, built and operated a political machine that delayed the re-turn of planter dominance for four years after Redeemers took over the state government. Campbell bound the freed people into a cohesive group whose unity led to a degree of self-determinism few blacks enjoyed during Reconstruction. Unified behind a goal-oriented leader and willing to use black power when necessary, McIntosh blacks gained rights, political positions, and capital, both in physical prosperity and what economists call "human capital," that other blacks only knew in their dreams. Blacks controlled the county's political economy and prevented the return of planter power until 1876, when the counterrevolution removed their leader from power.

In 1876 Tunis Campbell was sixty-four years old. For twelve years he had struggled to aid and direct the former chattels to become free people not only under the law— Union armies, the Congress, and the Constitution did that—but free-in-fact, free to think for themselves and to control their own destinies. In so doing, he made powerful enemies who finally conspired to bring him down.

At a time in life when most men count their blessings and list their accomplishments, Campbell found himself hired out under Georgia's convict labor system. Wearing striped pants and chains around his legs, this former state senator and judicial officer labored piling brush on T. J. Smith's Washington County plantation. Most white citizens of coastal

Georgia rejoiced at his humiliation. His black constituents despaired of their loss.[15] But before conspirators railroaded him from the state on trumped-up charges, Campbell made lasting contributions to the black community of McIntosh County. Those contributions and Campbell's persecution are the dual focus of this book.

CHAPTER ONE

SEPARATISM FOR STRENGTH

And I ain't going to get whipped any more
I got my ticket,
Leaving the thicket,
And I'm a-heading for the Golden Shore.

FRANK A. PATTERSON, 1865

Old Master's gone and the darkies stayed at home;
Must be now that the kingdom's come and the year for
jubilee.

FREEDMEN'S SONG

Tunis Campbell understood what had to be done when he arrived on St. Catherines Island in the final months of the Civil War. General William T. Sherman had just completed his march to the sea and was busy subduing remaining Confederate resistance in South Carolina. On the Georgia coast, former slaves, the contrabands of war, struggled to learn what it meant to be free from "chatteldom." They craved to experience freedom. Campbell had come to help them, and he had prepared well for the task. He knew how to deal with hostile whites, and he knew the desires of the freedmen.

His childhood in New Jersey had given Campbell more

contact with whites on an equal basis than most blacks experienced in nineteenth-century America. His father, John Campbell, a person of color, was a blacksmith in Middlebrook, New Jersey. Young Tunis and his nine siblings had the opportunity to see whites interact with their father in daily business situations.[1]

In 1817 a white friend of the family initiated Tunis's formal education by placing him in an Episcopal school in Babylon, New York, which he attended until he was eighteen. He later described the experience: "I was the only colored child in the school. The principal and assistants were very kind to me."[2] Spending twelve years in an almost wholly white environment, Campbell learned to deal with white people as a peer rather than as an inferior. His intellectual attainments surpassed those of most American whites and all but a handful of blacks. His comment about the kindness of the principal and assistants, however, suggests that his classmates and others may not have been pleasant to him. Nevertheless, the jeers and name-calling that probably occurred helped condition him for the verbal abuse he would receive forty years later.

Campbell's education prepared him for missionary work in Liberia. But while he studied he changed his opinion about the removal of blacks from America and centered his opposition on the American Colonization Society (ACS). Founded in 1816 by Henry Clay and others, the ACS acquired land in West Africa and financed the resettlement there of any black Americans who would emigrate. Although the effort succeeded in forming an independent Liberian republic in 1847, it failed miserably as a solution to slavery and race problems in the United States. Opposition came from free blacks who considered themselves Americans, not Africans; from southern planters who resented any efforts to interfere with the institution of slavery; and from the abolitionist movement of which Campbell was a part. Campbell vocally opposed colonization and undertook a lecturing campaign against slavery. He also converted to the Methodist faith and returned to his parents' home, now in New Brunswick, New Jersey. Campbell became radical in his views toward slavery and was convinced "never to leave this country until every slave was free on American soil— unless I went to . . . help secure their liberation." Preaching weekly in areas of New York City among "dens of thieves and pannel-houses [brothels]," he considered himself a "moral reformer and temperance lecturer." His social work spread to Jersey City, Brooklyn, and Williamsburg and included founding schools and churches for black people. In 1832 he established an anticolonization society in New Brunswick.[3]

Campbell worked hard in support of his race and became a popular speaker at rallies. On April 23 and 24, 1849, public meetings were held in New York City to oppose Liberian colonization. The *North Star,* an abolitionist newspaper owned by Frederick Douglass, reported that more than twelve hundred of the "most respectable and intelligent part of the colored people of this city" attended the first day's session. Among the seven speakers were Frederick Douglass and Tunis Campbell.[4]

At a meeting of 114 delegates to the Colored National Convention held in Rochester, New York, on July 6–8, 1853, Campbell played a key role, serving on the eight-man committee to nominate convention officers and on the finance committee and the committee on credentials. Convention organizers proposed establishment of a national council of colored people "for the purpose of improving the character, developing the intelligence, maintaining the rights, and organizing a Union of the Colored People of the Free States." Not wanting to exclude radical whites who wanted to help blacks, Campbell moved successfully to delete the word "Colored" from this preamble. Never antiwhite, he desired republicanism for all people and slavery for none. The convention denounced colonization by resolving "that as for the American Colonization Society, we have no sympathy with it, having long since determined to plant our trees on American soil."[5]

Campbell learned much from such conventions and meetings, including at least a rudimentary knowledge of parliamentary procedure. He heard speeches and made many himself, thereby growing accustomed to addressing large crowds. Participation in committee work, spirited debate, and procedural maneuvers would serve him well in the confused political situation in postwar Georgia.[6]

Campbell preached to as well as organized his fellow blacks whenever he could. But he also had to make a living. From 1832 until 1845 he lived in New York and worked as a hotel steward, the last three years as the principal waiter at the Howard Hotel. Then, for an undetermined period, he worked at the Adams House in Boston. While there, he wrote *Hotel Keepers, Head Waiters, and Housekeepers' Guide,* the first manual written by an American about the supervision and management of first-class hotels. Certificates of recommendation from his employer and patrons of the Howard Hotel appended to the text praised him as "universally esteemed . . . an unusually intelligent, dignified, attentive, and obliging man . . . of unblemished moral character, with a disposition to elevate the condition and character of persons of his color." The Adams brothers "found him courteous and polite . . . prompt and honest." During these years he interacted constantly with whites of all classes, and he apparently gained their respect. He displayed an aptitude for the organization and management of those who worked under him. In the preface to his book Campbell wrote, " 'Order is Heaven's first law,' it becomes our duty to aim at, if we cannot attain it, in all things." He would later need to recall these words and employ his organizational skills to the fullest.[7]

In 1861, Campbell again lived in New York, now with a wife, Harriet, and three children, one an adopted son. He volunteered to quit his job at a bakery and enlist in the army "to aid the Government in putting down the rebellion." But the United States at that time had no black soldiers and did not want any, so Campbell had to watch and wait. After Abraham Lincoln issued the Emancipation Proclamation on January 1, 1863, Campbell presented the president with a plan to educate and uplift the freed people of the South to relieve the government of its guardianship role. Lincoln ignored the petition. Undeterred, Campbell persuaded a New York friend to intercede in his behalf, and finally, at age fifty, he entered the employ of the nation in pursuit of a lifelong dream. Secretary of War Edwin Stanton commissioned Campbell to report to General Rufus Saxton, who was in charge of confiscating abandoned plantations and providing for the contrabands in South Carolina. Campbell would aid in the resettlement of freedmen.[8] According to Campbell, "I was sent down . . . to organize civil government, to improve the colored people in the South wherever I could do it, and . . . to instruct and elevate the colored race." With three or four thousand dollars of his own money he set out for Port Royal, South Carolina, in late summer 1863.[9]

Saxton had been at work at Beaufort and the Sea Islands since October 1862 under "carte blanche" orders to "take possession of all the plantations heretofore occupied by rebels and take charge of the inhabitants remaining thereon . . . with authority to take such measures, make such rules and regulations for the cultivation of the land, and for protection, employment, and government of the islands as circumstances may seem to require."[10] With the authority to do as he saw best and with no white southerners to hinder operations or inspire fear in the former slaves, Saxton wasted little time organizing his charges.[11]

Campbell benefited from his association with Saxton and

from his Port Royal experience. In New York, he had moved in radical circles but had limited opportunities to talk with former slaves. He had shared the platform with Frederick Douglass several times, had frequently conversed with this exceptional thinker and antislavery protaganist, and no doubt had absorbed and drawn upon Douglass's ideas. As a promoter and subscription agent for the *North Star* in New York, Campbell also had ready access to many abolitionist newspapers. Now in 1863 on the South Carolina Sea Islands, Campbell met hundreds of former slaves, some of them very recently freed, who told him about their experiences in bondage and expressed their hopes and dreams for the future.[12]

Besides his many conversations with the freed people, Campbell observed and interacted with numerous politicians, philanthropists, military leaders and soldiers, abolitionists, and missionaries. Among the more visible missionaries were the Gideonites, a band of reformers from Boston and New York led by Edward L. Pierce and Mansfield French, who had come to Beaufort in 1862. Campbell must have heard them exhort the blacks to work hard, learn to read and write, and live morally. By studying others as they ministered to the freedmen, he acquired ideas and methods to put to his own use.[13]

Campbell also observed many unprincipled opportunists who were drawn south by the Port Royal experiment hoping to make fortunes or to expand their power. He witnessed their misdealings and heard of abuses perpetrated against the former bondsmen. Of the many incidents of maltreatment and violence by individual civilians and federal troops, perhaps the most shocking happened just before Campbell's arrival. On St. Helena's Island in February 1863, men from several Union regiments killed animals, stole money, beat, and attempted to rape freed people. They burned cabins, threatened superintendents, and generally terrorized the population. A black woman reported that the victims "would be glad if all the white people would go away and let them live by themselves."[14] In the Sea Islands, black confidence in white men, even Yankees, waned, as Campbell must have heard from the freedmen with whom he talked at Beaufort and Hilton Head. And Campbell was not a man to ignore injustice, especially when perpetrated against members of a race he had spent so much time and energy trying to uplift.

In addition to educating the freedmen and encouraging self-reliance, the Port Royal experiment served as a training and recruiting ground for personnel of the postwar Reconstruction. Many years earlier, Campbell had in effect been in a "correspondence school," developing ideas, preaching liberation, and promoting self-reliance among blacks in the North. Now, working among the freed people in the South, he learned from firsthand experience. He developed confidence in his ability to help the freedmen. In 1865 he got his chance.[15]

In January 1865, William Tecumseh Sherman was a worried man. His army had just completed a bold modern strike through the heart of Georgia but had acquired a major problem—contrabands. Hordes of blacks freed by the army attached themselves to their liberators and created an enormous logistical problem. Not only did they slow military progress, but they became a severe drain on resources. Additionally, a hostile northern press increased the pressure on Sherman to do more to help these refugees. Something revolutionary had to be done soon.[16]

On January 12, Sherman sent a letter to his superior, General Henry W. Halleck, in response to criticism that he was doing little to help the contrabands and even refusing them the protection of his army. Critics asserted that Joseph Wheeler's Confederate cavalry had killed those blacks Sherman turned away. Sherman maintained that no refugee had been rejected and called the report of killings by the Confederates a "cock and bull story." Admitting that his column was "overloaded with two-thirds negroes, five-sixths of whom are helpless, and a large proportion of them babies and small children," Sherman promised, "I do and will do the best I can for the negroes."[17]

At eight o'clock that evening, Sherman, Stanton, and Assistant Adjutant E. D. Townsend met with a delegation of twenty Savannah black leaders. Garrison Frazier, a Baptist minister and the group's spokesman, responded to twelve prepared questions. His answers foreshadowed the action Sherman eventually took. Frazier said that "slavery is receiving by irresistible power the work of another . . . [freedom] is taking us from under the yoke of bondage and placing us where we could reap the fruit of our own labor and take care of ourselves." He continued, "The way we can best take care of ourselves is to have land," and we "prefer to live [in colonies] by ourselves." All but one of the representatives endorsed Frazier's statement.[18]

Four days later, Sherman issued Special Field Order No. 15, which he designed not only to relieve the army of its black followers but also to conform to Garrison Frazier's proposed program. It provided for the settlement of contrabands on an exclusive reservation made up of "the islands from Charleston south, the abandoned rice-fields along the rivers from thirty miles back from the sea, and the country" southward to the St. John's River. No whites except military personnel would be allowed to live on these islands or settlements, and blacks were given "sole and exclusive management of affairs." Settlers could claim a homestead of up to forty acres and receive possessory titles issued by the inspector of settlements and plantations, subject to presidential approval. Rufus Saxton was named inspector of settlements.[19]

Less than two months after Sherman issued Order No. 15, Congress established the Bureau of Refugees, Freedmen, and Abandoned Lands. General O. O. Howard was named commissioner. In recognition of his experience and proven abilities, Rufus Saxton was appointed assistant commissioner for South Carolina and Georgia.[20]

Saxton then appointed Campbell as superintendent of islands for Georgia. Campbell had previously been assigned as "governor" of five Georgia islands. He described his new position: "After the fall of Charleston I requested to be sent to the Sea Islands, in Georgia, and had assigned to me Burnside, Ausaba [Ossabaw], Saint Catherine's, Sapelo, and Colonel's Islands, with orders to organize and establish governments on the Islands, protect the freedmen and refugees for thirty miles back from the seashore." Saxton gave Campbell the authority to act on his best judgment in the administration of these lands.[21]

At about the same time that Robert E. Lee and Ulysses S. Grant met at Appomattox Courthouse to end the war, Campbell and a few families left Beaufort by boat to establish settlements on the Georgia islands. They stopped briefly at Hilton Head and Savannah to take on more emigrants bound for Sherman's promised land. Loaded "as deep as we could swim," the freedom ship made stops and unloaded hopefuls at Ossabaw, Delaware, St. Catherines, Sapelo, and St. Simons islands. Anticipating the freed people's needs, Campbell wrote a letter to the New York Freedmen's Relief Association asking for sweet potatoes, seed, and "all the clothing and books you can [send]." One week later, Campbell wrote that the settlers had enough food to survive, but again requested sweet potatoes to supplement their diet. He expressed hopes that they would make "a good crop of cotton," but he needed plows, cultivators, hoes, harrows, and lime. Lamenting the death of Lincoln and conditions in Georgia, Campbell wrote that "everything is in confusion."[22]

Indeed, coastal Georgia had been in a confused state since

the early days of the Civil War. Perched precariously on the seashore, the planters, other citizens, and slaves were vulnerable to attacks from the Union blockading and raiding ships, especially after the fall of Fort Pulaski in April 1862. Fearing for their safety, whites and their families took slaves and what property they could to safer areas in the interior of the state. By December 1861, most had evacuated the Sea Islands, and by the end of the summer of 1862, only widespread groups populated the coastal mainland.[23]

By 1865 the confusion had increased. In the face of revolutionary prospects for change, old thoughts clung tenaciously, and if there had to be change, most coastal whites preferred it to be reactionary. Freedmen and poor whites drifted from place to place looking for families, for work, for hope. The planters found themselves stripped of economic foundations and uncertain how to recoup their losses. In the midst of this disorder, Tunis Campbell established a colony based on the promise of Order No. 15 and the concept of "separatism for strength."[24]

Whether Campbell ever seriously considered setting up a truly separate black nation on the Sea Islands is unknown. Such action seems out of character with his anticolonization views and his attempts to lift his race to the republican equality enjoyed by whites. Yet his experiences at Port Royal must have dampened his hopes for biracial democracy. Surely he did not intend to establish a permanent separate black nation. Campbell did think flexibly and pursued his goal of equality by the most expedient route. In the spring of 1865 that route seemed to point to separatism. The freedmen needed time to grow, to be instructed in democratic ways, to develop a true feeling of equality, to learn self-sufficiency, and to establish nuclear families free from the watchful eye, instructions, and intimidations of still-hostile whites. Campbell believed that separation for strength was the quickest way to transform the freedmen into free men. Then, at some later date, not far distant, black free men could settle among white free men as equals. Campbell was not alone in his belief in the need for separation.

On May 22, 1865, General Saxton issued an enforcement order in which he warned that any persons violating any provisions of Sherman's Order No. 15 would incur the penalty of having "their effects . . . seized for the benefit of the freedmen, and themselves sent out of the Department, or otherwise punished." He ordered superintendents to display this edict prominently and to ensure compliance. Saxton promulgated this order specifically to keep speculators, promoters, and other fortune-seeking whites out of the lands promised to the former slaves. Of course, he permitted missionaries and military officers there.[25]

Settlement progressed rapidly despite some setbacks. The first reversal came in April, just two weeks after Campbell left Beaufort to begin colonization. The steamer *Enoch Dean,* in the employ of Saxton and bound from Savannah to the islands, capsized and sank in St. Catherines Sound. She had been loaded with freed people and their worldly possessions, as well as a large amount of seed and farming equipment desperately needed to grow crops for sustenance and market. The *Savannah Daily Herald* reported that all passengers and crew had survived, but much property was lost. Because of Saxton's transportation needs, the ship itself constituted the major loss.[26]

On St. Catherines, Campbell quickly displayed his ability as an organizer. By April 26, following his own admonition that "order is Heaven's first law," he established a government for the settlement, modeled after the United States Constitution.[27] Appropriately, he established his headquarters in the eight-room house of Button Gwinnett, a revolutionary firebrand of another era who had signed the Declaration of Independence. Cambell wrote an elaborate constitution, organized an eight-man senate and a twenty-man house, and set up a judicial system capped by a supreme court. Recognizing the need for the people to defend their newly gained freedom and property, he founded a militia company of approximately 275 citizen-soldiers. There can be no doubt that Campbell became "the autocrat of the island," but he was certainly well-meaning and benevolent. General Saxton had not ordered the establishment of a bicameral legislature and a court system governed by a constitution, nor did Port Royal provide the precedent for it. Campbell had determined to teach the democratic process. This functioning example of representative government would afford the former slaves a chance to experience firsthand the workings of republicanism and therefore help finish their conversion to freedom. Campbell busily prepared them for the future when they would vote.[28]

By June 16, Campbell had settled 214 adults and 98 children on Sapelo Island and 200 adults and 117 children on St. Catherines. He reported that the earliest settlers were self-sufficient, but those just arriving from the mainland still needed assistance. He requested ninety-eight first primers and forty spellers for the St. Catherines children's school, plus clothing, marriage licenses, plows, and hoes. By that request, Campbell revealed his understanding of freedmen's hopes and goals—education, individuality, family unity, and self-sufficiency. He predicted that by the end of July three-quarters of the St. Catherines settlers and one-half of those on Sapelo would be able to do without government rations. He expressed the hope that soon "their crop will be ready for market which will enable everyone to be self-sustaining."[29] Looking confidently to the future, Campbell suggested levying taxes on the freedmen to establish a school fund. A person afraid of failure or suspicious of a permanently indigent, dependent population could hardly have

suggested a progressive tax at such an early stage of settlement. Tunis Campbell steadily nudged the colony toward
black self-determination.[30]

To attain this goal with the greatest speed, Campbell felt
it necessary to bar all whites from the islands under his supervision, which he apparently felt Saxton's supplement to
Sherman's Order No. 15 gave him the right to do.[31] With
northern politicians debating whether the planters or the
freedmen had the right to the land and with the instability
in Georgia, Campbell seems to have been justified in his
efforts at separating blacks to gain strength.[32] When Union
sailors on federal gunboats harassed the people under his
charge, he threatened to "lock up the offenders" if it happened again. Perhaps remembering the abuses Union soldiers had committed at Port Royal, he was also aware of mistreatment of blacks in mainland McIntosh County, and he
wrote Saxton's military assistant, A. P. Ketchum, that "the
Planters on the ridge [four miles north of Darien] are treat-
ing these people very badly. They want protection."[33] Campbell intended the experiment in separatism on St. Catherines to continue just long enough to give the freed people a
chance to grasp at least a small handhold on the American
Dream. Reintegration into the white world depended on how
rapidly they gained strength and the white reaction to that
strength.

Campbell recognized that for the former chattels to be
free-in-fact, he must instill in each individual a sense of
purpose and provide each with some measure of political involvement, landownership, and education. They needed to
acquire both real and human capital—real in the sense of
land, property, and money; human meaning literacy, ego en-
hancement, ability, and knowledge. Campbell expressed his
own understanding of human capital as "brain and muscle."
By increasing their human capital, Campbell hoped to expand the people's opportunity to accept a diversity of jobs

and to grow intellectually secure. The freedman would be truly a free man because he could now compete for better jobs. And by being capable of understanding employers' and storekeepers' shares or account books, the free man protected himself against a variety of abuses.[34]

By organizing the militia unit and establishing self-government, Campbell inspired in his people a spirit of community cooperation. The militia unit would create an esprit de corps that would lead to a sense of obligation to protect the common welfare. Self-government would teach citizens' responsibilities and roles in a democracy and give the people a place to turn for redress of grievances. The Republic of St. Catherines was to be a true democratic republic.

Campbell wasted little time providing for education of the children. By June 30, 1865, he reported that eighty children on St. Catherines and sixty on Sapelo Island were enrolled in school. In August, using his own money to supplement that given him by General Saxton, he brought his son T. G. Campbell, Jr., from New York to assume management and supervision of the islands' schools. One month later Campbell reported to Saxton, "We cannot take anymore [students] at present as we have not got books for them. There are a great many adults who want to go also but we cannot take them." Soon thereafter, Campbell's wife and adopted son joined him, and they, too, began teaching. By January 1866, 200 to 250 children had enrolled in classes. Except for the initial funds from Saxton and the gift of books from benevolent missionaries in Savannah, Campbell carried most of the financial burden for teachers' support and school supplies. On April 11, 1866, when expenses had increased, he wrote the American Missionary Association pleading for money to build schools and buy supplies: "There are two schools wanted on Ossabaw, 3 on Sapelo, and 2 on Colonel's Island. We have 2 on St. Catherines with good teachers but want proper buildings. I have supported the 3 teachers and paid their way down. I find it a very severe task. I hope that you will consider our case, there are many calls upon you but none that merit your attention more."[35]

Campbell knew that for his charges to become truly self-reliant, they must settle on land of their own. He equated republicanism with Jeffersonian ideals. Simply to give freedom to blacks tossed these impoverished, illiterate laborers into a free-labor marketplace in which they could neither compete for jobs nor expect decent wages. Campbell believed the Radical Republican and Jeffersonian ideology, as described by Eric Foner, that "small farms, thrifty villages, free schools, . . . respect for honest labor, and equality of political rights" characterized the ideal democratic community. He believed that republican citizenship depended on control of productive property. Sherman's "reservation," Saxton's orders, and Campbell's implementation promised and seemed to be delivering land into the hands of the freedmen. Foner has called black Reconstruction a "stunning experiment." His argument that Radicals tied landownership to republicanism is borne out by Campbell's efforts on St. Catherines. Although self-sufficiency initially meant poverty and bad times, that was preferable to the alternative of virtual slavery under a white master. Land of one's own concomitantly increased real and human capital as farmers decided for themselves what to do, when to do it, and how to accomplish results. Freedom-in-fact stood nearby.[36]

By December 15, 1865, Campbell had settled or was in the process of settling 369 people on St. Catherines. On Ossabaw Island there were 78 settlers and on Sapelo 352. The Freedmen's Bureau provided rations to support refugees until they reached "settler" status. The system seemed to have worked. From an analysis of the rations received and issued on St. Catherines Claude Oubre concluded that "most of the Freedmen on St. Catherine's must have been self-sufficient, otherwise they might have gone hungry had they depended on government rations. He [Campbell] received and issued one-eighth barrel of salt, two barrels of meat, one-eighth barrel of sugar, one-eighth barrel of soap, five boxes of bread, three-fourths barrel of hominy, one-half cask of bacon, and one-fourth keg of vinegar. Obviously, these rations were not sufficient to maintain 369 persons."[37]

St. Catherines and the other Georgia Sea Islands averaged fifteen feet above sea level. Their sandy soil proved well-suited for growing long-staple cotton and diversified crops, including corn, sugarcane, fruits, melons, Irish and sweet potatoes, and a great variety of vegetables. Deer, rabbits, raccoons, wild boars, and game birds abounded, and trout, turtle, mullet, crab, shrimp, prawns, oysters, and clams could be found in the saltwater streams.[38] In 1878, the Georgia commissioner of agriculture reported, "I have seen no section of Georgia in which the people seem to secure a comfortable supply of food with less effort."[39] That abundance of food enabled the freedmen to survive on the starvation rations the Freedmen's Bureau provided. Additionally, they found many cattle abandoned by their former owners roaming the island, and they slaughtered the animals for food or sold the surplus meat with island melons and other produce at the Savannah market.[40]

As refugees arrived on St. Catherines, Campbell settled them into the fifty-four tabby or log cabins that had been used to house slaves in prewar days. These dwellings were concentrated in two communities—one on the north end near the Gwinnett house, the other three and one-half miles south. The south end settlement had at least twenty cabins. He provided the settlers with up to forty acres of land on which they could establish homesteads. By February 1866, he had parceled out land in varying acreages to approximately 425 freedmen and their families. The plots were scattered over the island, which tended to increase the freedmen's hold over the entire island and helped to discourage any outsider from trying to exploit the land or the freedmen in violation of Sherman's and Saxton's orders. It also increased the freedmen's sense of autonomy and allowed them to practice self-reliance by establishing and maintaining independent families and farms. This procedure worked very well initially because the transition to free labor occurred in the absence of the former masters. But no one could predict the planters' response to this black autonomy and alien free labor radicalism.[41]

The planters did respond. They wanted their lands restored, and they wanted the freedmen to work for them. Under presidential Reconstruction they would soon get their way. Jacob Waldburg, the prewar owner of St. Catherines Island, was among those wanting the land returned. In 1860 Waldburg was the largest landholder in Liberty County with nineteen thousand acres and second highest slaveholder with 255 slaves, controlling a total estate worth $383,000. On June 28, 1865, the *Savannah Daily Herald* reported that the military provost court had reviewed his application and had restored the land to his control.[42] General E. A. Wild, one of Saxton's subassistant commissioners, believed that the provost court had acted in error and intervened to prevent Waldburg's reclamation attempt. Wild wrote Saxton that St. Catherines "had already been laid out for division among Freedmen . . . [and] the alarm spread among negroes concerning the tenure of lands . . . is mischievous." Blacks were indeed alarmed. Wild reported that they feared they might not get land if they dallied: "With the utmost eagerness [they] did . . . apply for passes to the Islands . . . and with haste selected their plots of ground."[43]

Campbell continued to approve land grants and warned his charges against working for whites. He instructed them on the advantages of independent labor, telling them to let the whites take care of themselves. He reported to the Freedmen's Bureau that even when contracts could be made fairly with white men, "the facts are the men wanted to work for themselves." He knew that there would be an attempt to overturn the gains achieved, and he obviously knew that both southern white paternalists and northern capitalists would abuse labor for chances at quick fortunes.[44]

On an inspection tour of the islands in July 1865, Colonel J. S. Fullerton found Campbell to be "an intelligent and energetic colored man." He reported to Freedmen's Bureau Commissioner O. O. Howard that blacks had Ossabaw, St. Catherines, Sapelo, and other islands under cultivation and explained that "Gen. Saxton is and has been giving almost his exclusive attention to the Sea Islands, and his plan is to people and cultivate these in accordance with the Sherman orders."[45]

Shortly thereafter Howard decided he could best serve the freedmen by dividing the large area under Saxton's control into localized administrations. In August 1865, he left South Carolina and the Georgia Sea Islands under Saxton's care, but gave Florida to T. W. Osborne and put mainland Georgia under Davis Tillson. By this action Howard unintentionally hurt the freedmen he had intended to help. Whereas Saxton worked to implement revolutionary land redistribution and black rights, Tillson believed in a more conservative approach to modernization and reconstruction. He considered property sacred and thought it must be used to its fullest potential. That purpose would not be served by distribution to blacks, who, he believed, would work only under white supervision. Therefore, bureau-supervised labor contracts would achieve the most equitable arrangement between parties.[46]

At base, Tillson seems to have been concerned with helping the freedmen, but he was more interested in capitalist expansion and profits than with humanitarianism and radical reform. He would not tolerate paralyzed labor relations, nor did he have the patience for the time-consuming work of

ensuring an equitable readjustment between former masters and slaves. Under Tillson's guidance the contract system was employed as the most efficient way to get blacks
back in the fields, and the Freedmen's Bureau expedited the
restoration of black labor to the control of the former masters or to northern speculators.[47]

Tillson's policy conformed to President Johnson's program
of restoring land to the former owners, but Saxton's did not.
Whereas Saxton advocated radical land distribution leading
to fee-simple landholding for blacks, Johnson dictated the
return of the land to the former owners. Saxton opposed the
president's policy by refusing to restore any land for which
he had issued possessory titles. Finally, on January 1, 1866,
the president would tolerate his subordinate's obstructions
no longer. He fired Saxton and placed the Georgia islands
under Tillson's control. One month later Tillson made an inspection tour and was surprised to find that "there were no
white men on the . . . islands" under the control of Campbell and that "the freedmen were armed and would not allow any white person to land. . . . Influenced by Campbell,
the freedmen were unwilling to permit the white owners to
return to the islands, even to occupy such portions of their
property as had not been assigned to freedmen in compliance with General Sherman's Special Order No. 15. . . .
They had all the animals, implements, seeds, and nearly all
the food, required to enable them to make a crop this year."[48]
Campbell had provided well; separatism for strength was
working.

But Tillson would not tolerate this experiment in black
self-determination. He used federal troops to force the
freedmen's militia to give access to whites. He immediately
reprimanded Campbell and began his policy of forcing
blacks without valid land claims into labor contracts with
whites under terms he deemed satisfactory. "Should such
freed people refuse to accept the offer thus made, then they

shall [be] remove[d] from such plantation, and allow the owners thereof the opportunity to hire others to cultivate the same," he declared.[49]

Two northern capitalists, John F. Winchester and Schuyler had rented a portion of the Waldburg plantation on St. Catherines Island. Prodded by Tillson and against Campbell's advice, 147 freedmen signed contracts with them. Those who signed most likely came from a pool of 200 new arrivals who had no land. Destitute and afraid, they had not yet come under Campbell's influence. Another 475 freedmen on St. Catherines continued to work for themselves. Tillson approved only seventeen land grants, declaring the majority of those belonging to blacks who refused to sign contracts to be invalid. Further, he reduced the acreage granted and consolidated the grants to one portion of the island, leaving the remaining acreage to the northerners.[50]

Tillson became increasingly convinced that Campbell was a negative influence on the freedmen and an obstacle to his authority over them. In his November 1866 report, he predicted that the freedmen working for Winchester and Schuyler would make a cotton crop "three times as large as that raised by the freedmen." Tillson neglected to take into account the difference in resources between the northern speculators and the freedmen, the freedmens' proven lack of interest in growing a crop they could not eat, and the northerners' use of the effective, though slavelike, gang labor system, whereas the independents worked their own small plots.[51]

Tillson failed to mention that the freedmen cultivated eighty-five more acres of corn than the northerners. They probably had larger crops of all foods and a more diversified diet of meat, game, and fish than did those working for Winchester and Schuyler. Tillson seemed to think acreage planted and cash crops constituted the only barometers of success. The independent freedmen gained more than simply the cultivation of cash crops. They accumulated human capital at a greater rate than did the hire-outs. They supervised their own labor, made decisions on a multitude of farm problems and situations, witnessed failures and successes among their peers, saw leaders emerge, and lived in "collective autonomy." These personal experiences were vital if the freedmen hoped to gain equal shares in the bourgeois revolution started by the Civil War and continued by Charles Sumner, Thaddeus Stevens, Howard, Saxton, and Campbell.[52]

Tillson increased his assaults on Campbell until he could manufacture an excuse to discharge him. An incident concerning the island's timber provided such an occasion. Apparently, Saxton had given Campbell permission to cut wood and sell it to passing steamers. When Tillson heard of the matter, he confronted Campbell. Just as in the case of the land grants, Tillson doubted that Saxton had given Campbell authority to cut and sell wood. Further, he charged that Campbell had not paid some of the freed people for their labor and insinuated that Campbell had pocketed the money from the sales. He charged that in other cases freedmen "had been paid in whole or in part in intoxicating liquors and that no account had been rendered the Government for the proceeds of the wood." Campbell countered that he had asked Saxton "what tax this would be upon the People if they cut wood and sold it" and that Saxton told him "to let them cut and get what they could for it." Therefore, no proceeds were due the government. R. K. Scott, who replaced Saxton in South Carolina, could find no records of this case; when relieved, Saxton had taken everything with him. Nevertheless, Tillson declared Campbell guilty of misconduct and discharged him.[53] Whether Campbell pocketed the money himself, kept it against debts owed, had not yet paid it out, or held it to pay the bureau for rations remains a mystery, although it seems highly unlikely that a minister of

the African Methodist Episcopal church and a temperance
lecturer for more than thirty years would have given liquor
to anyone.

Although no longer a bureau agent, Campbell remained
in coastal Georgia and advised the black people "to live
peaceably among themselves." His family continued to
teach at the St. Catherines school, although enrollment
dropped from 150 students to 60. Campbell took time to attend the Georgia Education Association meeting in May,
and the delegates elected him vice-president in recognition
of his organizational abilities and educational work. He
made trips to Sapelo and the mainland encouraging freedmen to think and work toward independence.[54]

About the same time that Winchester and Schuyler as-
sumed control of St. Catherines, two other speculators,
McBride and S. D. Dickson, leased Sapelo from the Spalding
estate for $2,500 a year. Although they contracted to pay the
freedmen on very liberal terms—two-thirds of the crop—
these freedmen did not want to work for whites. Many of
them had remained on Sapelo when owner Randolph Spalding left in 1862. They had faith in Sherman's promise of
land, and for them separatism for strength was working. By
1865, Freedmen's Bureau agent W. F. Eaton reported that
130 of them were self-sustaining, 100 nearly self-sustaining, and 122 new arrivals in need of support. By December
1, most of these had become self-reliant, having "raised
enough produce to supply themselves almost wholly."[55]

That same month, Freedmen's Bureau Commissioner O.
O. Howard's brother, C. H. Howard, made an inspection tour
and reported that the "900 colored people upon Sapelo . . .
intended leaving the island in case one of the former
owners . . . returned to resume possession." When forced to
choose between working for McBride and Dickson or leaving, however, most signed labor contracts. This proved to be
a mistake. When it came time to settle up, the speculators

did not fulfill the generous terms they had originally offered.[56]

McBride and Dickson established a store so the freedmen could obtain items on credit until settlement could be made at harvest time. An innovation, the plantation store provided merchandise to the worker and reduced the capital outlay by the planter. Because the freedmen wanted "civilized goods" but had no money to buy them, this system seemed expedient. But many planters charged excessive prices and took advantage of the former slaves' arithmetical inability to cheat them mercilessly. The temptation to defraud the freedmen proved irresistible for most speculators, whose reason for coming south had been to strike it rich. Freedman Toby Maxwell had been working for the speculators when the Sapelo crop was harvested. He remembered that as they figured accounts against the piles of cotton the freedmen brought in, McBride and Dickson said "they owed them nothing . . . the cotton was taken. Some of the col'd men refused to put their cotton in McBride's pile. He then had them arrested and carried to Ft. Pulaski."[57]

Tillson reported the incident to Howard and said that he had arrested "12 of the ringleaders and confine[d] them in Fort Pulaski where they will be kept at hard labor until such times as they shall have made up their minds to return to the island and conduct themselves as becomes peaceful law abiding citizens." He explained that fairness compelled him to arrest the freedmen because Dickson and McBride had acted as furnishing agents at his request. Tillson "felt it my duty to interfere to protect them against loss." As further justification he noted that the blacks had been complaining about the injustice of their contracts and were refusing to recognize their validity. He blamed Campbell for this dissatisfaction and the resulting trouble.[58]

When Generals James B. Steedman and J. S. Fullerton made an inspection tour in 1866, Tillson told them that

Campbell had exerted an evil influence over the freedmen and had unscrupulously "bought their cotton at 10 cents a pound in the seed and paid them mainly in whiskey." Remus Elliot, a freedman on Sapelo and witness to the events, testified that Campbell had helped the blacks there and "was not connected with any cotton combination nor attempts to defraud the Negroes nor had anything to do with it." Historian William McFeely's research indicated that the inspection tour was part of an overall conspiracy by President Johnson, Fullerton, Steedman, Tillson, and others to discredit the Freedmen's Bureau in favor of the planting interests. Elliot's affirmation of Campbell's honesty is no doubt correct. And Tillson was partly right—Campbell did have influence with the freedmen.[59]

Typically, Tillson had protected capitalists and contracts instead of the rights of the freed people. He considered Campbell's teachings the main impediment to getting the freedmen to sign and be satisfied with their labor contracts. Campbell was the firebrand inspiring resistance to authority. As a remedy, Tillson issued Special Order No. 130, which provided that "the Rev'd Tunis G. Campbell, [colored.] late Agent of this Bureau, at St. Catherine's Island, having been found guilty of dishonest practices [granting land, selling timber, opposing contracts] and removed, and there being good reason to believe that he is advising the freed people on Sapelo Island, to pursue a course alike unjust to their employers, and injurious to themselves, is hereby forbidden to visit Sapelo Island on pain of being arrested."[60] Campbell realized that if he wanted to continue his work, he would have to relocate his people, and he decided to find a place on the mainland.

By December 1866, Campbell had become convinced that the freedmen would not obtain land or justice from Davis Tillson; yet he determined to continue his efforts in their behalf. In mainland McIntosh County, fifteen miles south-

west of St. Catherines, a northern sympathizer, C. H. Hopkins, Jr., agreed to sell land to Campbell for $14.50 an acre.
The plantation BelleVille, located on the south bank of the
Sapelo River, contained 1,250 acres. In good faith, Campbell
advanced $1,000 of his own money and apparently agreed to
make installment payments of $5,000 until the remainder
was paid. Under this early version of a rent-to-own agreement, the freedmen would pay a yearly rent of one-third of
the harvested crop of corn and cotton and make installments
toward outright ownership. Obviously, Campbell believed
land ownership was necessary to raise the freedmen and remained determined to obtain it. Initially, for Hopkins, the
agreement provided financial salvation from the devasta-
tion of war. Later, he would have a change of heart and
would get the courts to restore the land to him.[61]

Campbell went to Augusta and requested Tillson's permission and protection to go to the islands to move some of
the dissatisfied freed people to BelleVille plantation. Tillson
refused to assist him in any way. Campbell then hired a sail-
boat to take him to the islands. He quickly picked up those
who wanted to go with him, and in a flotilla of small boats,
which included the schooner *Amelia,* they sailed or rowed to
BelleVille. On arrival they found no houses excepting the
charred remains from Civil War fires. Using old boards and
palmetto branches they built huts to provide immediate
shelter. Evidently, they trusted Campbell implicitly and believed in his admonitions with enough conviction to start
over again in the wilderness. Testifying in 1871 before the
congressional committee investigating Ku Klux Klan activities, Campbell summed up the freedmen's hopes and his
own answer to their needs: "The great cry of our people is
for land. If they can be protected they will get on well
enough. . . . They want to be free-holders, land-holders, and
to hold office like white men."[62]

Campbell wanted blacks to join the mainstream of bour-

geois American society. He knew that with land of their own
and time to become accustomed to freedom they would be
able to advance rapidly. That was the theory behind the separatism for strength experiment on St. Catherines. Now at
BelleVille, there was still a chance for growth through
quasi-separation. Campbell would continue to use this tactic
until circumstances opened for advancement by other means.
The impulse to live separately clashed with the impulse to
integrate into the American mainstream, but for the time
being, separatism was the best tactic.[63]

On January 14, 1867, C. C. Sibley replaced Davis Tillson
as the assistant commissioner for Georgia. Campbell surely
rejoiced at the news, and perhaps in celebration wrote a letter to Howard asking for assistance for the BelleVille freedmen. Howard returned the letter and instructed him to contact Sibley, whom he had instructed to aid BelleVille.[64]

With the promise of rations secure, Campbell turned his
attention to organizing the colony. Because solidarity was a
key to success, he organized the nascent community into an
association devoted to the common good. On March 4, 1867,
he wrote a constitution that provided a governing structure,
established offices, listed rules, and expressed hopes for the
future.[65]

Campbell organized the BelleVille Farmers Association to
function much like a city government. He provided for
elected officials—president, vice-presidents, treasurer,
secretary, sheriff, deputy sheriff, constables, fence mender,
road master, market inspector, building janitor, and hog and
cattle reeve. The treasurer was to keep a strict account of
monetary transactions. Apparently Campbell wanted to ensure that no question might arise over money collected from
each farmer and repaid to the Freedmen's Bureau for debts
owed or rations. He instructed the secretary to correspond
with other groups and record the workings of the association
"to demonstrate to all [the] feasibility of this plan of working

and to show the people of this State and Country that we can be, are, and with Freedom will be a producing tax-paying element." Law enforcement officers would maintain the peace and association employees were charged to ensure the good working order and cleanliness of communal property. The market inspector was to inspect all meat and produce sold in the community to help control disease.[66]

Campbell and the members of the association agreed to act for the good of the community. Each family would control its own land but would reap the benefits of an extended family relationship. To demonstrate their commitment to this compact, members agreed as follows: "We hereby pledge ourselves, our interest[s] and our labor to the successful issue of this the permanent [organization] for our welfare and hope thereby to merit the approbation of our friends who have assisted us and the disappointment of our enemies who seek our downfall."[67] Campbell's adopted son, E. E. Howard, predicted: "Soon will this place teem with the fruits of the people's labor and . . . this land, now almost impenetrable with weeds and underbrush, having grown up so profusely during the year, laid out into little farms of from ten to twenty acres, and what is better still, the people who thus labor will be able to claim it as their 'home,' where, under their own vine and fig tree they may contemplate the goodness of God."[68]

The freedmen chose Campbell as president of the association and business agent for the colony. As members they withheld the right to appeal directly to the Freedmen's Bureau in case of any dispute between Campbell and the colony. Campbell had thus ensured the rights of the freedmen, even against abuses which he might knowingly or unknowingly perpetrate against them.[69]

By June 1, 1867, Campbell had settled sixty-one adults and forty-seven children on BelleVille lands. Beginning in May, the Freedmen's Bureau had provided rations for the colony totaling $1,050.47. Itemized, this total consisted of $371.81 for May, $321.39 for June, $284.32 for July, and $72.95 for transportation costs. At harvest time, the total amount was to be repaid with each farmer providing an amount in proportion to the supplies his family had received.[70]

The weather did not cooperate; 1867 was almost as bad a crop year in McIntosh County as 1866. One planter stated: "In 1866 our crops were almost a total failure by reason of drought. In 1867 the crops were drowned, we had 105 successive days of rain. . . . Where I had been accustomed to gather forty bushels of corn per acre, the past year [1867] I gathered about four, that of inferior quality."[71] At Belle-Ville conditions were the same; Campbell reported that "we got along very well until the Heavy Rains Came in July which damaged the whole crop of *Cotton* and *Corn*."[72]

The BelleVille residents were also required to do more than planting and harvesting crops. It had been six years since the fields had been cleared and prepared for planting. Additionally, the settlers struggled until May, when the first Freedmen's Bureau rations arrived, to provide food and shelter for their families. They spent much time hunting, fishing, and gathering forest products to eat and firewood to heat their huts. Still, the twenty-six families planted 436 acres—336 in food crops and 100 in cotton. It was not enough to offset the debt for rations, the rent due Hopkins, and the amount necessary to stockpile food for the winter. The freedmen's desire to become autonomous farmers able to concentrate on growing subsistence crops was counteracted by the need to grow marketable products, if for no other reason than to pay the rent and reimburse the Freedmen's Bureau. Campbell attempted to achieve both by suggesting the number of acres of corn or cotton each farmer should plant. When weather or worms interfered to upset the delicate balance between subsistence and commodity crops, the security that the freedmen and Campbell strived for was jeopardized. Part of becoming independent entailed selecting one's own crops and resisting growing cotton and rice, the crops of slavery, but failure to grow enough marketable crops endangered the status blacks wanted to achieve.[73]

From the sale of the cotton, the freedmen repaid $552.63 on their debt to the bureau, but because they had not repaid the entire amount, subassistant commissioner J. M. Hoag of Savannah reported "the enterprise an entire failure . . . scarcely enough [had been made] to settle for rations." He reported that seventy-five hundred pounds of cotton and four hundred bushels of corn had been harvested and attributed the poor crop to caterpillars and idleness. He had learned of the idleness from "statements of disinterested neighbors." Hoag failed to take into account the conditions the settlers had faced upon arrival at BelleVille and the progress they had made. The freedmen's first concern had been survival, and their progress had been impeded by bad weather and the lack of capital to invest in working animals and tools. The "disinterested neighbors" had merely mouthed the beliefs of most whites that "you cannot make the negro work without physical compulsion" and expressed the desire to see the black enterprise fail.[74]

Campbell realized that the colony could do better, and he remained realistic in his expectations, writing to Hoag: "The people have not done as well as might be expected in a more promising season, but have I think done as well as possible taking into consideration the cotton worm and inauspicious weather. We are however hopeful of success and still determined to use every effort to give a favorable termination of affairs."[75]

Ever an optimist, Campbell looked forward to the future. He proposed to add twenty-four more families to the twenty-six already at BelleVille. He told Georgia Inspector General

J. R. Lewis that the freedmen trapped wild hogs and chickens to supplement their primary diet of fish, turtles, and oysters. Campbell suggested that each family be required to plant three acres each of corn and cotton to pay the $5,000 in installments to Hopkins. He continued counseling the people to "quietly live and work for their living."[76]

Apparently, Campbell clung to the idea that separatism for strength provided an environment more conducive to the freedmen's success than living among the unreconstructed white southerners or unprincipled northern speculators. For two years he had worked with the Georgia freedmen encouraging, helping, and directing them toward free-in-fact independence. He had been successful in providing the instruction by which they gained in human capital, and he still hoped that the BelleVille homesteads would provide real capital gains.

In the Congress of the United States, Radicals busily implemented revolutionary programs that would give him the chance to obtain statewide prominence in the Reconstruction movement. McIntosh County was about to undergo an experiment in black self-determination through militant black power politics.

CHAPTER TWO

NEGOTIATION FROM
STRENGTH

We only want our share of the turkey—nothing more,
nothing less.

HENRY M. TURNER, 1874

y 1867, Radicals controlled the United States Congress and brought an end to conservative presidential Reconstruction. The time to transform the
freedmen into free men—politically, socially, and
economically—would never again be so propitious. On March
2, over President Johnson's veto, they enacted the First Reconstruction Act, "An Act to Provide for the more Efficient
Government of the rebel States." This act divided the South
into five districts, instituted martial law, and enumerated
prerequisites for readmission to the Union. On March 23 and
July 19, Congress again overrode the president and passed
two supplementary acts. Under federal guidance, the people
of each southern state had to register all qualified voters,
hold a referendum to elect delegates to rewrite state constitu-
tions in compliance with the U.S. Constitution, elect state
governments, and ratify the Fourteenth Amendment. In
Georgia, Tunis Campbell played a prominent role in fulfilling
these requirements; in so doing, he altered his position on
black separatism.[1]

He still believed that the freedmen could at first advance faster outside white society; but he was now willing to try mediation to achieve equality. With the Democrats in control of Georgia politics, there had been no chance to enforce equal treatment; but now, with the Radicals in charge, negotiation from a position of strength might uplift the black race and provide more equal treatment and advancement opportunities. Campbell tried to use congressional Reconstruction to force whites to accept racial equality.

At the BelleVille community, Campbell was busy working as adviser and agent to the freed people. He surely delighted in the news that blacks would be registered and then allowed to vote; he had long preached on the necessity of this step for complete independence. He also realized that for the freed people to grow, they must have time to solve their own problems without his daily leadership. He had never wanted to replace "Ole Massa" as patriarch in a paternalistic system. Campbell wanted each freedman to become self-reliant, truly a free man. Besides, he was struggling to uplift a race, not just a few of its members. Johnson's Reconstruction plan had stifled that chance, but now Congress had opened the door for genuine reform. Campbell decided to seek political office to further black rights.[2]

Opportunity came in the form of two military orders. General John Pope, commander of the Third Military District (Georgia, Florida, and Alabama), issued Order No. 5 (April 8, 1867) and Order No. 20 (May 21, 1867) implementing procedures to register voters in compliance with the March 23, 1867, Act of Congress. For each of Georgia's senatorial districts, he selected a three-man board of registration made up of one black and two white citizens. For Georgia's Second District—McIntosh, Liberty, and Tatnall counties—Pope appointed James Rahm, T. P. Pease, and Tunis Campbell.[3]

To encourage the registration of as many eligible voters as possible, Pope proposed to pay the registrars fifteen to forty cents for each voter registered. In McIntosh County, they signed 675 blacks and 128 whites to the voting rolls. Campbell quickly grasped the potential of this four and one-half to one advantage of black voters for advancing his work to the state level.[4]

As he registered voters, Campbell advised the freedmen of the power of the ballot and pointed out that the Republican party had been responsible for their freedom. Pope's orders to the registrars had included instructions for them "to explain to all persons, who have heretofore not enjoyed the right of suffrage, what are their political rights and privileges, and the necessity of exercising them upon all proper occasions." The need for instruction was apparent. Yet there can be no doubt that as he carried out this duty, Campbell built upon his reputation as a talented speaker to gain an advantage in upcoming elections.[5]

While being involved in the registration process and maintaining his position as agent for the BelleVille settlement, Campbell drew upon his tireless energy to attend several conferences promoting black rights and to make many speeches exhorting blacks to be vigilant. At a mass political conference in April, Campbell encouraged the freedmen to seek education and called on Pope to expedite registration and elections. Campbell wanted educated black voters at the polls as soon as possible.[6]

Although Campbell traveled and spoke throughout the state, his performance at an April 15 Republican meeting in Darien provides a good example of his tactics. After delivering the opening prayer, he made an hour-long speech in support of Radical Reconstruction. An opening prayer was the norm for political meetings, but in this case it became more than simply an invocation of God's assistance in the proceedings. Black preachers held considerable power in their communities. When a preacher combined prayer with politics, the politics often became a religious experience in the minds of the audience. It may have been different if the preacher and politician were different people; but in this case, Campbell the preacher became Campbell the candidate. It seemed to follow that God guided the rally through His mouthpiece —Campbell. His influence among the freedmen soared. Following his performance at Darien, the *Savannah Daily Republican* reported that Campbell fully satisfied the gathering "with his superior language and the logic of his deductions." He had "expressed himself satisifed as to the manner that all would use the ballot in McIntosh county" and predicted that the ballot would remove unjust laws, promote the dignity of labor, and make Georgians "a united happy people."[7]

On May 1, 1867, Campbell attended the Georgia Education Convention in Macon, for which he had helped prepare the agenda. To acknowledge his efforts in support of black education, the delegates elected him vice-president. They resolved to establish local educational associations, promote education, and seek out and employ qualified teachers in their localities.[8]

During the week of June 15–20, Campbell participated in a regional conference of the African Methodist Episcopal Zion church in Augusta. An elder in the church, he threw himself into the daily sessions, won election as a corresponding editor for the national church paper, *Zion Standard and Weekly Review,* and participated on at least five committees. He firmly supported the need for more education and called for more day and Sabbath schools. Knowing the advantage of having a correctly informed citizenry, another Jeffersonian tenet, Campbell joined other conference members in recommending that all present should read the Radical organ the *Augusta Daily Loyal Georgian.* During closing ceremonies Campbell took a prominent role in drafting the conference's final expression of purpose—a hope to bind all Methodists together in a Christian march toward equal rights. Drawing upon Lincoln's Second Inaugural Address and anticipating sermons by Martin Luther King, Jr., one hundred years later, the statement declared: "We will pursue the right, as God gives us to see the right, trusting that the dawning of a better day has begun to show itself, in which all the differences of the past shall be forgotten . . . we will ever preach a gospel of peace and good will to all mankind."[9]

Indefatigable and ubiquitous at meetings aimed at advancing black rights, Campbell became one of the state's leading Radicals and a prominent member of Georgia's Union Republican party. He served on the State Central Republican Committee, but whether he helped construct its platform is unknown. The several planks endorsing congressional Reconstruction, calling for the establishment of free public schools for all children, declaring the dignity of labor, and supporting equal rights for every Georgian reflect his views.[10]

On Independence Day he represented McIntosh County at the Republican State Convention in Atlanta. The delegates elected him vice-president for his conspicuous efforts in support of Republican programs. One newspaper reporter at the convention wrote: "The colored men of the Convention . . . met the whites on equal ground, feeling that it was no disgrace to be black. They argued well and showed themselves men of ability and task. Take, for instance, the conduct of Mr. Campbell, who won favor everywhere, than whom none was more honored and respected . . . [and who was one of] the leading spirits of the Convention." Campbell had established himself in state politics.[11]

In the ensuing five-day election, October 29 through November 2, McIntosh County voters elected Campbell to represent them at the Constitutional Convention. He was one of 37 blacks among the 170 delegates elected statewide. Boycotting the election, no whites voted in McIntosh County;

but the result would have been the same had all eligible whites supported a conservative candidate. Campbell's efforts to improve the condition of freed people and his considerable oratorical talent had unified a local black majority in his support.[12]

At the convention, Campbell, Henry McNeal Turner of Macon, and Aaron Alpeoria Bradley of Savannah were the three most prominent blacks. Turner was born in South Carolina in 1834 of free black parents. He moved to St. Louis in 1857, then to Baltimore, then Washington, D.C. An elder in the African Methodist Episcopal church, he became America's first black army chaplain in 1863. As did Campbell, Turner worked among Georgia blacks as a Freedmen's Bureau agent and, later, with Radical Republicans as an organizer. From 1868 to 1872 he served in the Georgia legislature as a spokesman for black rights. After the counterrevolution put Redeemers in power, he urged blacks to leave America to the whites and emigrate to Africa. Aaron Alpeoria Bradley, born into slavery of a black mother and a white father in South Carolina, escaped to the North while still in his teens. He returned to the South after the Civil War and organized Savannah blacks into a powerful political force. Unlike Turner and Campbell, who presented level-headed arguments against reactionaries, Bradley spouted hateful bombasts against white conservatives. All three strongly promoted landownership, citizenship, and suffrage for blacks.[13]

Contrary to reports in the conservative press, the tone of the convention was only moderately radical. Republican ranks split between moderates and radicals. The white delegates, though mostly Republicans, still had to return home to face their white neighbors; they would not concede too much to blacks. Also, most of the black delegates had been prewar bondsmen, and they remained somewhat intimidated by whites and tended toward accommodation. Campbell, Turner, and Bradley actively sought reform, but their political inexperience and naiveté led them to put too much faith in their fellow delegates and misuse what little numerical power they had. Bradley vocally stormed for black rights, but his stubborn refusal to compromise and his abusive protestations resulted in his expulsion. The votes of Campbell, Turner, and the other blacks made his expulsion unanimous, probably as an act of good faith and a sign that they were willing to mediate.[14]

Records of the proceedings indicate that Campbell attended every session of the three-month convention. His attendance record reflects both a fascination with politics and his belief in democratic government. He naively felt that discrimination could be legislated away. He was more active behind the scenes than on the floor, but he did make important contributions. On the first day of the convention, December 9, 1867, Campbell introduced a resolution requiring that all candidates for the convention presidency define their position, but no one seconded the motion. The next day he unsuccessfully made the same resolution, adding that he wanted to know each candidate's position on aid to the freedmen and on black suffrage. He also called for the removal of everyone but delegates from the convention hall so that the deliberations might proceed in an orderly, dignified manner without interruption or intimidation from onlookers; that motion was tabled.[15]

On December 16, Campbell offered a resolution to abolish imprisonment for debt in Georgia. The law on the books clearly discriminated against and exploited black labor by putting debtors in state work camps. The resolution passed and became a part of the constitution. Later, continuing his assault on prejudicial practices and seeking social reform, Campbell called for a law to stop unequal treatment on public conveyances. He cited a case in which two black men had been refused first-class passage on a steamer and had been forced to ride in the open with the freight, segregated from white passengers. He had been one of those men. The convention delegates voted to bind this resolution over to the first meeting of the General Assembly for action.[16]

As a member of the Committee on Education, Campbell promoted schooling for all children. He proposed that Article One of the new constitution should include the sentence: "No discrimination on account of color or previous condition shall be made in this State," but he accepted an alternative statement stipulating that all Georgia citizens be entitled to equal civil and political rights and public privileges. When G. P. Burnett of Rome proposed a resolution that Georgia was and forever would be governed by white men, Campbell jumped to his feet and implored the convention to show the world its condemnation of such measures. Burnett withdrew the resolution before a vote.[17]

When Bradley argued that many blacks were being unjustly held in the state's prisons, Campbell proposed that the military commander of the Third District investigate the charge and release all illegally held prisoners. He also opposed any alteration of the loyalty oath required of voters and officeholders. The oath required that before being seated, each senator, except those pardoned by the president of the United States, swear that he had never voluntarily taken up arms against the United States, held Confederate office, or aided or encouraged anyone who did. That "test oath" helped establish a barrier to the resurgence of planter power, and Campbell wanted as many barriers as possible. Throughout the session Campbell acted as a watchdog for black rights.[18]

On the important matters of debtor relief, the "black" officeholding clause, and the franchise report, Campbell's record is mixed. His resolution to abolish imprisonment for debt was tied to the ordinance that nullified debts contracted before June 1, 1865, so he voted yea for debtor relief. In an effort to restrict the franchise, John E. Bryant, a white Radical who represented Augusta and edited the *Daily Loyal Georgian,* tried to amend the suffrage bill to exclude from registration or officeholding all those disqualified by the Fourteenth Amendment until Congress restored their rights. Campbell helped vote down this amendment, probably believing it unnecessary because the Fourteenth Amendment took precedence. He also voted against a clause that would specifically give blacks the right to hold office. Campbell felt strongly against such delineation by race. To add the term "negro" and specifically to confer rights on a segment of the population opposed his understanding of equality. His decisions on these issues resulted from his political naiveté and immaturity as well as a misplaced faith that white Georgians, especially legislators, would follow the intent of the Fourteenth Amendment.[19]

The convention completed its work by drafting the most liberal constitution in Georgia's history. It ended imprisonment for debt, gave suffrage to black men, and provided a public school system for both races. Campbell's activity in state politics thrust him among the black leadership, and from his seat on the State Central Republican Committee he helped determine strategy for party programs. With the April ratifying and general election coming up, Campbell had much to do.[20]

Campbell supported the constitution and campaigned for the state senate. He vigorously promoted the Republican party in McIntosh, Liberty, and Tatnall counties during the month before the election. He entered the senatorial race and supported his son, Tunis Campbell, Jr., for the House of Representatives. Throughout the Second District, blacks recognized Campbell as the black man who had registered the freedmen. With an established public image and his previous election to the Constitutional Convention, he entered the race as the "incumbent." The nearly two-to-one black

majority of registered voters in the district did not hurt
Campbell's cause (see Table 1).

This time the whites registered and voted instead of with-
holding their ballots as they had in the vote on the Constitutional Convention in 1867. But it made little difference.
Georgians ratified the constitution and elected the Republican Rufus Bullock as governor. Tunis Campbell became a senator, and voters elected his son as the representative for McIntosh County. Liberty County voters also elected
a black representative, William Gaulden. Tatnall's white
majority resulted in a white representative, Robert Sur-
rency, but the black majorities in McIntosh and Liberty
counties overrode votes for John B. Gordon and William
Robert Gignilliat and against the constitution (see Table 2).

Voters elected Campbell as one of only three blacks chosen for the senate and picked his son as one of twenty-nine
blacks in the house. In the senate, Campbell sat on the Committee on Petitions and the Committee on Education. He
was one of two senators to join with two representatives as a
delegation to notify Governor Bullock of the legislature's
readiness to receive his address. That selection reflected his
high standing among the Radicals.[21]

TABLE 1. VOTER REGISTRATION, 1867–1868

	Blacks	Whites	Total
McIntosh County	713	164	877
Liberty County	874	294	1,168
Tatnall County	146	478	624
Totals	1,733	936	2,669

*Source: Report of Madison Bell, Comptroller General of
the State of Georgia, Covering the Period from August 11,
1868, to January 1, 1869* (Atlanta: Samuel Bard, Public
Printer, 1869), Table A.

TABLE 2. ELECTION AND REFERENDUM, APRIL 20–30, 1868

County	Governor		Ratification		Senator	
	Bullock	Gordon	For	Against	Campbell	Gignilliat
McIntosh	446	135	460	124	*	*
Liberty	711	145	714	143	*	*
Tatnall	78	184	140	219	*	*
Totals	1,235	564	1,323	486	1,256	539

Source: Report of Madison Bell, Comptroller General of the State of Georgia, Covering the Period from August 11, 1868, to January 1, 1869 (Atlanta: Samuel Bard, State Printer, 1869), Table A; Senate Journal of Georgia, 1868, p. 326.
*Information not available.

Campbell worked indefatigably in the senate. Proposing to revise the judicial system, he introduced a bill to provide for the selection of intelligent jurors in criminal cases and to pay them adequately. He continued the assault on discrimination by public carriers that he had begun in the Constitutional Convention; his bill, entitled "an Act to Compel Common Carriers to Provide Equal Accommodations for Passengers without Any Discrimination," asked more than "separate but equal." He also introduced a bill designed to improve black mobility by incorporating "the Georgia Steam Navigation Company, for the transportation of passengers from BelleVille to Darien, Brunswick, and Savannah." Senate committees adversely reported all three bills, and all lost by senate vote. Campbell's programs were too revolutionary for his colleagues, but even in legislative defeat, he proved himself assertive and independent—the ablest black in the senate. His activities belie the myth which Margaret Mitchell perpetuated in Gone With the Wind: "These negroes sat in the Legislature where they spent most of their time eating goobers and easing their unaccustomed feet into and out of new shoes."[22]

Conservatives abhorred the black presence in the legislature and wanted them removed. They especially resented the seating of A. A. Bradley, who had been expelled from the Constitutional Convention for abusive language and immoral conduct. Senator Milton A. Candler of Washington unsuccessfully entered a resolution against all three black senators, arguing that the constitution did not grant blacks the privilege of officeholding.[23]

Campbell immediately protested this resolution and began a defense of black eligibility. Of the three black senators, he argued loudest and longest. His July speech on the eligibility question appeared in the center column of the front page of the *Atlanta Constitution*. Campbell declared that blacks were unprotected in Georgia because of the "great evil" of discriminatory practices and that he wanted only to do what he had been elected to do—protect and further black interests. He declared blacks eligible to hold office and spoke of the injustice of trying to expel them. He "appealed to the hearts of the members . . . [and] he hoped the gentlemen would act without prejudice, [and] deal fairly with himself and his friends." Though sincere, this appeal reflected his failure to understand southern whites' uncompromising attitude.[24]

Campbell sat on the five-man committee appointed to investigate the charge that Bradley had been convicted of seduction in New York—a felony—and was therefore disqualified from the senate. By a vote of three to two, this committee found Bradley guilty as charged and recommended his dismissal. Campbell presented the minority report arguing that Bradley's guilt had not been established beyond a reasonable doubt, that seduction was not a felony in New York or even a crime in Georgia, and that one's behavior in another state or country had little relevance to affairs in Georgia. Campbell then filibustered for three days in Bradley's behalf. But Bradley's race was the real reason for his removal, and the senate forced him to resign.[25]

One month later, the Georgia General Assembly culminated its assault against nonwhite members. On September
12, 1868, following the similar expulsion of blacks from the
House of Representatives, the senate, by a vote of twenty-
four to eleven, decided that blacks had no right to hold office
in Georgia and expelled Campbell and George Wallace, senator from the Twentieth District (Hancock, Baldwin, and
Washington counties). Surprisingly, after the vote, the senate allowed Campbell's protest to be heard and recorded in
the *Senate Journal:*

> You have this day decided by your vote, declared us not
> eligible to seats on this floor.
>
> Sirs, by a very large majority of all the votes cast in our
> several districts, and by the right guaranteed us both in
> the Constitution of the United States and of the State of
> Georgia, as well as in the Reconstruction laws of Con
> gress; we claim to be the legally elected Representatives of
> a very large portion of, and nearly one-half of the legal
> electors of the State of Georgia.
>
> Sirs, the Constitution and the laws of Georgia strictly
> provide that no law shall be made or enforced which shall
> abridge the privileges or immunities of citizens of the
> United States, or of this State, or deny to any person within
> its jurisdiction, the equal protection of its laws.
>
> Therefore in behalf of ourselves, our constituents, and
> also in behalf of nearly five hundred thousand loyal cit
> izens of this State, we do enter our solemn protest against
> the illegal, unconstitutional, unjust, and oppressive action
> of this body, based on the resolution of the Senator from
> the 35th Senatorial District, declaring us ineligible on ac
> count of color.
>
> And we respectfully request that this, our protest, be
> spread upon the journals of the Senate.

Following Georgia law, the candidates who had received the
second highest number of votes in the election replaced

members expelled from the legislature. Darien attorney William Robert Gignilliat, a Democrat who received fewer than one-third of the district's votes, replaced Campbell.[26]

The afternoon of the senate's action, Campbell called a meeting of the expelled legislators of both houses. They decided that the Campbells would go to Washington to lodge a protest and to seek to prevent the seating of Georgia's United States senators. In Washington, they met with Senators E. D. Morgan of New York and Charles Sumner of Massachusetts. Campbell asked for a law protecting all persons regardless of race or former status. He claimed that this discussion generated the Fifteenth Amendment—"The right of citizens of the United States to vote shall not be denied or abridged by the United States or by any state on account of race, color, or previous condition of servitude." This language is indeed close to Campbell's proposal in the Constitutional Convention that "no discrimination on account of color or previous condition shall be made."[27]

After nearly five weeks in Washington, Campbell and his son returned to Darien around the end of October 1868. Earlier that year, Campbell had purchased property and built a house in Darien, probably moving his family from Belle-Ville because of his new position in county government. In the April 1868 election, voters had not only elected him to the state senate but also to the local office of justice of the peace. Darien was a city in transition, and blacks realized the need for a strong local official who would protect their interests.[28]

In 1863, the Fifty-fourth Massachusetts Regiment had burned the town, leaving only a few of the more than one hundred original buildings intact. Darien was too important to commerce to be long desolated, however, and by 1868 restoration efforts were proceeding rapidly. In 1870 Darien's population included 435 blacks and 111 whites, a radical change from the town's composition in 1860 of 255 blacks

and 315 whites. Most of the whites now lived four miles
north of Darien at "The Ridge," a high spot of land that had
been used as a refuge when the Union blockade began to
threaten the coastal areas in 1862.[29]

After the war, most southern whites had nothing but land
and the freedmen had nothing but freedom. Few of either
race had money. Many of the former slaves stayed on plantations when the war ended, trading labor, their only asset, for
shelter and food. In 1860, McIntosh planter Norman Gignilliat, uncle of Campbell's senatorial successor, sat near the
apex of southern society. He owned at least 152 slaves, fifth
highest in a county of wealthy aristocrats. Upon emancipation, he told his slaves that nothing had changed. They had
only themselves; he had land. He sent them into the rice
fields saying, "Roll up your sleeves, get back in the fields,
make me one hundred bushels of rice, and I will give you one
hundred acres of land." Land served as currency until economic conditions stabilized. McIntosh County historian Bessie Lewis recalled talking to an old man who had been very
wealthy during the war but had had to resort to trading
evenly—acres of land for bushels of sweet potatoes.[30]

Owing to the dearth of money, many people employed the
barter system to transact business in Reconstruction Georgia. One missionary teaching in Darien reported "taking
rice, potatoes, etc. in payment." Myrtie Candler of Newnan
described the system: "I got shoes in this way: we would send
four kid skins to the tanner. He would keep two skins for his
toll and give us back two . . . dressed skins. We would take
these two . . . to the expert shoemaker who would make me
a pair of shoes . . . from the leather of one skin, and keep
the other for his pay."[31]

The freedmen realized the necessity of obtaining their
own land if they were to be independent and free-in-fact.
Some gained landownership by the barter system, some
through the gifts of benevolent former masters, some
through wills, and at least three had turned extra money

over to their masters before the war to buy land which they now claimed.[32] But most freedmen had no choice but to live on land belonging to their former owners and hope for ownership—soon.[33]

To get land of their own, the freedmen had first to obtain money. Then they had to find someone willing to sell to them, which proved difficult because even with conditions as bad as they were, most planters refused to sell to blacks. The idea of blacks as independent farmers conflicted with white southern ideology, which held that blacks were not capable of independence. Status as independent farmers raised black standing on the social ladder, certainly against the wishes of most whites. Additionally, once a black got land of his own, the labor supply diminished by the number of hands in that family. The population density of McIntosh County was below the state average, so land was relatively abundant but the value of labor was correspondingly high. Frances Leigh of Butler's Island admitted that most "gentlemen" refused to sell land to blacks. Still, as soon as they could, blacks left the plantations and settled—"squatted"— in the piney woods. There they built cabins for their families, scratched out an acre or two to cultivate food crops, did odd jobs to supplement their income, hunted and fished and picked berries to supplement their diets, and lived in impoverished autonomy. They did not require large acreages; small plots were the rule. The acquisition of land raised a freedman's status because success was measured in independence from white control. This independence allowed blacks to control the hours and use of their labor.[34]

But it was difficult to obtain land, and various forms of tenancy often substituted for title. Most blacks started as wage laborers and struggled to advance up the agricultural ladder from sharecroppers to share tenants to fixed-payment renters to owners. The higher up the landed ladder one progressed, the more independent one became. Even the lowest rung, sharecropping, as Eric Foner has explained, "offered blacks a degree of control over their time, labor, and family relationships inconceivable under slavery." Blacks wanted to work for themselves and objected to the wage labor contracts that put them in labor gangs reminiscent of prewar days. Labor gangs tended the great staple, rice, which with cotton constituted the chief crops of slavery. Overseers assigned the tasks to be accomplished, and blacks had little control over their labor.[35]

By growing crops for shares, most McIntosh County blacks obtained a quasi-proprietorship over the soil. By 1868, three-quarters of all the contracts in the county were based on the share system. Not only did this system give blacks some freedom from white planters and a sense of landownership—and at least some control over the use of their labor—it also gave the planters more laborers. Women who had withdrawn from the labor force to establish nuclear families returned with their children to the fields during planting and harvesting to increase the share. The planter also benefited by sharing the loss of a poor crop with the laborer, which had proved difficult if he paid wages. But blacks tended to benefit the most from sharecropping, especially in the first few years after emancipation. Sharecropping or higher positions of tenancy gave them some control over their lives. Those who did not share the white middle-class notion that time is money could more actively pursue closer family ties, improve their station by learning to read and write, go fishing, attend meetings, or undertake a plethora of activities unavailable to a wage laborer who worked hours set by the planter.[36]

Campbell understood the people's need for land. He had been fighting for property rights since his early days on St. Catherines. Now, in McIntosh County, he worked actively to change the hiring and working system from one of coercion, with its inherent racism, intimidation, discrimination, and dishonest account keeping, to competition in an open market. Campbell wanted each worker to maximize his returns by getting the highest wage or share possible. He saw the contract as a great evil because it bound a laborer to a white employer and could be altered and reinterpreted to deprive workers of just returns. Contracts usually contained clauses allowing deductions for work that did not meet par, and the white employer determined "par." The laborers sometimes found the employer "mean" or working conditions not as promised, but they were bound to the agreement for its duration, usually one year. Campbell wanted to teach the freed people that labor was dignified and should be sought and appreciated. He believed in the free labor system and in American capitalism, but his strong humanism demanded fair treatment of workers. Blacks also had to overcome their fears of working for a "massa," which would be impossible if whites continued to cheat blacks through contract misdealings. Campbell knew that any tenant relationship between blacks and whites had the potential for coercion reminiscent of slavery. He well remembered the exploitive contract practices of Davis Tillson, Winchester and Schuyler, McBride and Dickson, and similar "devils" on the plantations around Darien.[37]

Campbell frequently called the McIntosh County blacks together to answer questions on labor relations or to counsel them on contracts. He advised them to be careful when they entered agreements because if they violated the work clauses, they could be sentenced to jail. He told them to make short contracts, preferably by the day, week, or month, so that they could extricate themselves from unfair or dangerous situations. If they did sign, they should work hard and "stick up to it . . . [because] their interests were identified with the whites." Campbell's object was not to prevent labor contracts from being made or to keep whites from getting the labor they needed, but only to ensure that the freed people understood the ramifications of such agreements and got the best terms obtainable.[38]

The McIntosh planters saw Campbell's frequent meetings
with the laborers as disruptive and costly. W. R. Gignilliat
claimed that Campbell's counsel to the freedmen was "a det-
riment pecuniarily to the tune of two hundred thousand dollars per annum." Frances Leigh described the planters' attempt to make Campbell compromise his principles "and
induce him by heavy bribes to work for us, or rather to use
his influence over our negroes to make them work for us."
They soon realized that Campbell was not a man to be
bribed.[39]

The planters tried to use alternative labor sources to rid
themselves of their dependence on blacks. Mrs. Leigh bought
a planting machine as "the first step towards freeing ourselves from negro labourers." She also entered into a scheme
to employ Chinese workers on McIntosh plantations. As a
part of this plan, A. S. Barnwell brought in thirty coolies to
work General's Island. Then, in a final attempt to overcome
Campbell's influence on the workers, Leigh brought eight
Englishmen to Butler's Island, but they proved to be poor
laborers and demoralized the black workers by leaving the
fields before completing their assigned tasks—an indication
of the difficulty of the work. Finally, only two choices remained. The planters would either have to deal more fairly
with their workers or dispose of Campbell. They knew that
while he retained influence over blacks in the making of
labor contracts, they would have to acquiesce to demands or
lose their laborers.[40]

Certainly, Campbell refined his ideas about labor contracts during his experience in Georgia among the freedmen. Yet as early as 1848 in his book on hotel management,
he had discussed proper labor-management relations and
the dependence of each on the other: "It is necessary to
make the interests of the servant and the proprietor one.
And both parties must feel their identity. Thus a mutual
good feeling becomes established; the interest of one be-

comes inseparable from the other; and the result is confidence and mutual dependence." On the importance of fair wages, Campbell wrote: "I must here mention one great error, and that is, the hiring of cheap help. The very best of help should be procured, and a reasonable compensation paid them for their services. They will then look to their employer for pay, and not be the whole time striving and planning to defraud him of an hour or two, that they may make a little extra to help out their wages."[41]

Campbell empathized with the laborer and resented anyone who failed to treat him fairly. He respected each individual's worth as a creature of God and therefore due the respect of his fellows. If he had been fighting for black rights in the North, he would have encountered white men attempting to squeeze out profits but with experience dealing with hired labor. But in the South, residual racism compounded the problem because whites continued to believe that blacks belonged to them. Campbell confronted a way of life and entrenched attitudes that war and law had altered little. He worked hard to protect the freedmen, according to his understanding and philosophy of labor relations. In 1877, when Campbell wrote of his experiences in Georgia, he began with that philosophy: "Those whose capital, given to them in brain and muscle by the Great Ruler of the Universe, has been ignored and trampled under foot by the moneyed aristocrats of this nation; for while it is eminently proper that each individual should be protected in all their lawful rights of property, yet they should never have any paramount claim on that ground over any other person."[42]

This statement summarized the problems involved in raising a race. Not only did Campbell believe in the rights of property and the promise of the American Dream, which meant that all people could justly aspire to become rich, but he knew the conflict of interests entailed in the search for wealth. He also demonstrated his belief that human capital should be held equal with real capital. Campbell argued that no claim to property could be tolerated in a democratic republic when it decreased another's rights. By 1877, Campbell realized that in the class conflict under way in the South between planting and laboring interests, the former had won, and he lamented: "No matter what might be the moral worth or respectability of a mechanic or laboring man, his interests or rights must not stand in the way of the wishes of the capitalists or property-holder. . . . How long will it be before you will have no rights that the capitalists or property-holder is bound to respect?"[43]

Campbell insisted on the worth of each person, whether born rich or poor. He condemned unprincipled capitalists for exploiting labor simply because they owned the means of production, and he declared that ownership of property granted no inherent rights. Campbell believed in the equality of all people and that all should be treated with respect. He hoped to persuade McIntosh citizens to deal fairly with one another and to settle their differences for the sake of mutual self-interest. To do this, he had to forge the black community into a cohesive organization that took advantage of labor scarcity, diverse occupational choices, and opportunities for educational advancement.

In Darien other agencies and individuals also tried to help the freedmen. In 1867 and 1868 the Freedmen's Bureau operated a dispensary under the care of Dr. T. L. Harris, who ministered to whites but mostly to blacks. The Freedmen's Bureau, northern philanthropic organizations—most notably the American Missionary Association—and private individuals operated schools in McIntosh County. A white teacher consolidated the schools Campbell established on St. Catherines into one school in December 1866. Campbell reinstituted classes at BelleVille in March 1867, with two teachers and seventy-five students. By May 1867, at least one other school operated in the county.[44]

The American Missionary Association (AMA), with the invitation and support of the Freedmen's Bureau, began sending missionaries to Darien in 1868. Annie Wilkins taught eighty day students and a large night school. Through May 1870, the AMA had at least two teachers in Darien instructing black children during the day, their parents at night, and all ages in Sunday school. Missionaries consistently reported that the blacks eagerly wanted to learn to read and write, that the whites opposed northern teachers and would not furnish living accommodations for them, that the black scholars learned quickly, and that the people suffered from poverty and found it difficult to pay for their schooling.[45]

A letter from AMA teacher Susan P. Harrold to her home office in New York reveals much about everyday conditions in Darien and indicates why the freed people needed someone like Campbell to stand up for their rights. She wrote that the children could "read any number up to billions—add and subtract and are now multiplying by two and three figures. . . . Many walk three miles to school. . . . The people here are generally very poor. They work mostly on rice plantations and are paid in orders on stores in which their employers are usually interested. They see very little if any money—many think themselves fortunate if they do not come out in debt to the establishment—much is ofttimes the case. . . . They are shamefully cheated."[46]

In addition to the missionary teachers, independent black teachers worked in Darien at different times, and it is likely that literate blacks helped teach others. The 1870 census lists eight private schools in McIntosh County with 9 teachers and 294 students. Progress was slow. In 1867 and 1868, 758 of the 879 blacks and whites who registered to vote could not sign their names. Projecting that 86 percent illiteracy rate to the total population, probably 3,854 of McIntosh's 1870 population of 4,484 could not read or write. Initially, daily education for all but the smallest children was out of the question because when it came to learning or starving, learning went the way of the rice chaff.[47]

In 1870, blacks predominated in McIntosh County by 3,288 to 1,196 and held a four-to-one majority in Darien. The 1860 census had listed 4,063 slaves, 54 free blacks, and 1,429 whites. The number of whites dropped primarily because of Civil War casualties. The black decrease undoubtedly resulted from shifts to urban areas, in this case Savannah, and the desire to escape the scene of bondage. In 1870, 1,453 people, one-third of the total population, were under eighteen years old. There were 2,218 males and 2,273 females, and at least 713 of the county's 972 males over the legal voting age of twenty-one were black.[48]

From his position as justice of the peace, Campbell wielded political, social, and economic power over this black majority, and as an elder in the AME church, he influenced them by sharing his ideas with them. He became spiritual overlord, labor adviser, black rights defender, and daily counselor to the black population. Black county officials—sheriff, ordinary, superior court clerk, constable—who had won elections on his coattails in 1868 made up part of his organization. Additionally, blacks held the registrar and city marshal positions, and by 1872 they controlled two city alderman seats, an election manager spot, and the coroner's post.[49]

Campbell used this political strength to mold the black majority into a community that understood that supremacy at the polls led to a more equitable social and economic climate. Blacks who gained elective office immediately moved into the county bourgeoisie and became part of a black elite. Whites had no choice but to consult them when problems arose. Black cohesion did much to frustrate the white coercive politics that controlled freedmen in other parts of the South. The black power structure confronted white planter interests to help shield blacks from some of the more exploitive practices of agricultural labor.[50]

Economically, blacks gained in McIntosh County because of competitive bidding for scarce labor, Campbell's efforts to make labor contracts fair, and diverse occupational choices. The Altamaha River and the Atlantic Ocean were the keys to this diversity. In Darien, timber quickly replaced rice as "king." Working with timber offered a chance to get out of the rice fields, and by 1870 blacks held sixty-seven of the seventy-six jobs for sawmill workers in Darien.[51]

Each year thereafter, the timber industry provided more and different jobs that enabled blacks to climb the socio-economic ladder away from agricultural laborer status. Darien began to grow, with its shops and saloons catering to the timber crowd and to the raftsmen who floated giant cypress and pine logs to the port city. Opportunities opened in the building industry, and there were new positions for dock workers, stewards, draymen, and jack-of-all-trade day laborers. In every case, blacks gained. A breakdown of black occupations in 1870 reveals that most workers still labored in agriculture, but increasingly jobs became available in other areas (see Table 3). Most women worked in the home taking care of their families. Others worked as domestic servants or in similar service jobs. Although one cannot be certain, it is likely that these housewives entered the fields to support their cropper-renter-owner husbands when the need arose.[52] But primarily, black women, with the overwhelming support of their men, worked in their homes as wives and mothers.

Campbell set up a separate social and political community in the county with its own ideological base. He taught blacks to question and to resist practices of their employers that they found abusive. He preached that "if they expected to be respected they must respect themselves." He encouraged them to get married and to shun immorality and infidelity. He advised peace between the races, obedience to just laws, and appeal to the courts for redress of grievances. He chal-

TABLE 3. BLACK OCCUPATIONS, 1870*

	Darien†	McIntosh County
Housewife	300	324
Farm laborer	173	263
Farmer	118	138
Domestic servant	81	52
Sawmill worker	58	9
Day laborer	50	30
Carpenter/brick mason	33	13
Porter/waiter/steward	15	1
Laundress/washerwoman	9	0
Seamstress	6	0
Drayman/teamster	5	0
Stevedore	5	0
Raftsman	4	0
Blacksmith/wheelwright	3	1
Hostler	2	0
Engine builder	2	0
Railroad worker	2	2
Schoolteacher	1	2
Barber	1	0
Pilot	1	0
Other	7	2
Totals	876	837

Source: U.S. Census, Population Schedule, McIntosh County, 1870.
*Does not include those listed "at home" or "at school."
†Darien figures include "The Ridge" and are not included in McIntosh County numbers.

lenged blacks to work conscientiously and to save their money so that they might buy homes for themselves and their families. He extolled a puritanlike ideology of self-reliance, lawfulness, piety, and hard work.[53]

McIntosh blacks advanced because of the county's diverse economy and their numbers at the ballot box. But Campbell's indomitable spirit and sense of mission led the way. His experience as a Freedmen's Bureau agent and his expulsion from the Georgia Senate in 1868 made him more determined than ever to extirpate racism and gain black rights. In McIntosh County blacks knew they could get justice in Campbell's court, and that knowledge gave them somewhere to turn if whites "pushed too hard."[54]

Campbell's political machine relied on grass-roots organization. He formed a citizens' militia company headed by a captain and a sergeant to protect blacks' rights. It resembled the better-known Union League clubs. When Campbell called the people together for political meetings, the militia organization passed the word throughout the county. Assistant Marshal Hamilton Jackson, a black man, testified before a Georgia Senate committee investigating Campbell's actions that "he very frequently calls the colored men off the plantations."[55]

Frequent meetings had two results: they pulled the black community into a tighter organization, and they increased Campbell's polity as the leader of this political machine. Blacks experienced a growing sense of racial solidarity and community identity. By accepting Campbell's pronouncements as their own, they gradually rejected planter hegemony. No longer would they bow to white "superiors"—politically, economically, or socially. Lieutenant J. H. Bradley, a white officer, heard one of Campbell's speeches and noted the crowd's reaction to it. His comments emphasize the authority Campbell had usurped from the planters: "They gaze upon him as a being having no part in their humanity, a demi-god whose wonderful attributes are quite beyond their comprehension and whose wisdom is past finding out, and they almost worship him and follow whithersoever he leads."[56]

Undoubtedly, whites viewed Campbell as an "uppity nigger" whose actions were merely histrionics. His charisma did enhance his status, but blacks clung to him because his efficacy and faithfulness to the cause of equality affirmed their belief in him. More than a "demigod," this revolution-

ary enjoyed extraordinary success among coastal blacks. He
had learned to inspire large crowds in New York City in the
1840s when he participated in the campaign against relocat-
ing blacks to Liberia. Literate and capable, he could with-
stand white vituperation. A powerful speaker, he cogently
articulated biting criticism of discriminatory acts, thereby
enamoring himself to blacks. His words expressed his understanding and belief in the same goals the freedmen held.
He had a sonorous voice, and he spoke in a precise manner to
emphasize his ideas. In 1870, at fifty-eight years of age, he
represented inchoate black power. As a preacher of the gospel, Campbell drew people to him as he spread God's word.
In his role as justice of the peace he demanded the respect
due that office. As head of the only organized militia force in
the county his word commanded strong-armed youths. Un-
questionably, his service as Freedmen's Bureau official,
agent for the BelleVille settlement, registrar of voters,
member of the Constitutional Convention, and state senator
increased his power over black bodies and minds. In addition, his 160-pound, six-foot frame towered over most of his
contemporaries. Giving strength to his appearance, his gray
hair and goatee framed an extremely black face. Brass-
rimmed glasses added dignity and a learned look. One Democrat, while writing passionately against Campbell, still
conceded that he was "commanding in appearance" with
"the faculty of attaching the masses to him in a most wonderful degree." A white superior court judge described
Campbell as a "most dignified and senatorial looking person." All this, plus his idealism, efforts for equality between
the races, and membership in the Republican party gave his
speeches great meaning among his people. No doubt many
saw in him a role model to emulate; he represented the truth
of the American Dream. Campbell did have a charismatic
following; but he sustained that charisma with concrete actions, attempting to lift blacks to autonomy in a bourgeois

society. He loved politics, but his first thought was always his black constituents. When forced to choose between actions that endangered his physical freedom or compromised the best interests of his people, Campbell chose to suffer in their behalf. He was a powerful politician—similar to a latter-day Huey Long or Adam Clayton Powell. Opponents charged that his success stemmed from excessive charisma. They were wrong. Campbell did have "presence," but his actions spoke louder and blacks loved him for that.[57]

On December 22, 1869, after hearing testimony about the Ku Klux Klan and other intimidation and discrimination cases against blacks, Congress reinstituted military rule in Georgia. Governor Bullock fought hard for this and drew support from a petition signed by seven hundred McIntosh County citizens who requested enforcement of the Reconstruction Acts. Additional support came from the lobbying efforts of Campbell and Foster Blodgett, a white Augustan who became one of Bullock's principal allies, who went to Washington on behalf of the Georgia Republican Central Committee to support Bullock. Campbell remained in Washington working for reinstitution of martial law until the act passed.[58]

When the Georgia legislature met on January 10, 1870, the new military commander, Alfred H. Terry, restored the black legislators to the seats they had lost in 1868. The legislature now had a Republican majority, but Campbell was incensed to see many Democrats who had falsely sworn the required oath still seated in obvious violation of the Constitution. As the senators were sworn into their seats, Campbell protested against those who had engaged in the rebellion or had held Confederate office and had not been pardoned by the president. He challenged seven of the forty-four senators. Benjamin Conley, president of the senate, accepted the protests but allowed the senators to take their seats. Campbell considered this action intolerable. After the day's adjournment, he filed complaints with Bullock and Terry. Terry ordered a board to investigate these charges, and on January 29 he purged six ineligible senators. Only three of these were among the seven against whom Campbell had brought protests, but he was essentially responsible for all the deposings. Campbell had made the 1870 senate more radical.[59]

With the exception of March and June, the legislature met every month during 1870; Campbell attended and actively participated in all sessions. As in 1868, he was a member of the joint committee to report the legislature's readiness to Governor Bullock. He took his familiar seat on the Committee on Education and sat on three other committees—Petitions, Penitentiary, and Military.[60]

Campbell introduced fifteen bills and resolutions designed to improve the condition of blacks. He hoped to effect judicial reform so as to make the law more accessible to blacks and to involve them as jurors. This would do much to protect their rights as citizens and help them toward greater freedom. He introduced bills to define the eligibility of jurors, to legalize juror selection in McIntosh County, to establish district courts in each Georgia county to stop the judicial process in state courts until reorganization was complete, and to require the Tatnall County ordinary to hold office in Reidsville, a location more accessible to the people.[61]

To upgrade the social, political, and military positions of his race, he offered bills to implement a nondiscriminatory system of public education in Georgia, to use immediately the money from railroad profits for education as provided by the constitution, and to change selection procedures for the commissioners of the McIntosh County Academy. He successfully moved to incorporate the Seaboard, Skidaway, and Pine Island Railroad. He convinced the senate to amend the acts incorporating the city of Darien to make them conform to the current constitution and to strike the words "white," "colored," or "negro" so as to make no reference to race. He offered a bill to invest the governor with the authority to raise and equip integrated militia companies.[62]

Campbell's belief in the power of the ballot and his intention to make sure that all blacks had access to it are evident in his Savannah bill, which amended the Georgia Code thirteen times relating to the state's largest city. Campbell wanted to eliminate the registration fee and establish more polling places to ensure that every voter had the opportunity to cast a ballot. In previous elections white election officials had crammed many voters into one room to create a situation that prevented blacks from entering to cast their votes. These officials did not think more polling places necessary, even though the state's other large cities provided many voting precincts. They pointed out that the courthouse was large and had four entrances and argued that more voting places would lead to election fraud, charging that on previous occasions South Carolina blacks had voted in Savannah elections. Campbell replied that no one protected the vote of the colored man in Savannah and that the authorities had used police forcibly to obstruct entrances to the courthouse so as to not allow blacks inside. In response to the comment about four entrances, Campbell said, "If the room were inadequate, of what use would be twenty entrances?" The bill passed the senate, even though Democratic papers referred to Campbell as "the Congo Senator" and his arguments as "the gorilla's insolent harangue."[63]

During the March adjournment, Campbell, his son, and nine others traveled to Washington to oppose the Bingham Amendment, a plan to readmit Georgia under a government of its own with elections to be held in the fall. Radicals feared that the instant the U.S. government declared Georgia reconstructed, reactionary whites would assert power and black gains would evaporate. Republicans wanted more time to consolidate achievements into lasting accomplishments. On March 12, Senator Hiram Revels of Mississippi, the only black United States senator, read a protest from the Georgia legislators that asked the Congress to kill the Bingham bill and requested legislation to "secure the passage of such jury laws as will insure justice to the colored man; of a bill for the promotion of education among all classes, and also such amendment of the election laws as will give a fair, free expression of each citizen's political views." The requested legislation was almost identical to bills Campbell presented in the Georgia Senate that year. During its attempts to influence amendment of the bill, the Georgia delegation met with President Ulysses S. Grant and Vice-President Schuyler Colfax. Campbell was now acquainted with the most powerful politician in America—a fact of importance later on.[64]

On February 1, 1871, delegates to the State Convention of Colored Men in Atlanta elected Campbell vice-president. President H. M. Turner appointed him to the Business Committee as well as to a committee to prepare a speech for the convention. The next day, in an opening speech, Campbell said that blacks must "move wisely, carefully, steadily, [but] without compromise. We must act in harmony with all acts in behalf of liberty." His thinking was again in transition. The continuing failure of efforts to propel his race toward equality and the Democratic majorities in both houses in the December 1870 state elections made him aware of the need for recalcitrance.[65]

During the afternoon session on February 2, Campbell proposed the establishment of a central Judicial Committee "to insure protection and enforce our rights." The convention named him president of that committee and resolved that it would consist of seven representatives from each county to be chosen by the county legislators. Whether that committee ever met is unknown, but the resolution's sentiment is evident. Campbell had become more militant.[66]

In other business, Romulus Moore, Columbia County representative in the state legislature and former member of the Constitutional Convention, stated that blacks could not receive justice in Georgia and should emigrate to the "promised land"—Arkansas. Campbell made an impassioned appeal against this proposal: "I propose to sink or swim, live or die, right here, and not ask any man if I can stay here. Let our wives and children know they have husbands and fathers [and] that we are able and willing to defend them in this State. I am opposed to any and all plans of emigration. I repeat, sink or swim, live or perish, Georgia is to be our home."[67] Thirty years earlier Campbell had fought against the American Colonization Society. Now, he similarly declared that blacks should live on their own soil—Georgia soil—as free people and not be forced to move to a "foreign" land, either in Africa or in Arkansas. His words, to "live or die" and to "defend" black interests suggested a new militancy. The delegates returned Moore's appeal to the committee. They also sent Campbell back to Washington to lobby for a law to protect all citizens of the United States against abuses. In Washington, Campbell met with Grant with unknown results, but his efforts and other evidence helped persuade Congress to pass the Ku Klux Act on April 20, 1871.[68]

Campbell returned to Darien determined to protect black rights. He no longer believed compromise would settle difficulties between the races. His long and trouble-filled experiences with whites transformed his plan to uplift his people. When he first arrived in Georgia, he strongly believed that for blacks to reach real independence, they must be allowed to establish farms of their own, learn to read and write, form nuclear families, and in all ways expand their human and real capital. To accomplish those goals as quickly as possible, Campbell established the colony on St. Catherines, based on separatism for strength. He organized a militia and began a self-governing structure for the freed people. When President Johnson and federal troops halted that experiment in black self-determinism, Campbell, still believing in separatism, purchased BelleVille and reestablished his colony. When Radicals surged to national power and instituted congressional Reconstruction, Campbell came to believe that whites and blacks might be able to coexist while the blacks gained self-reliance. He reasóned that with Radicals controlling national and state governments, the prospects for black advancement were better than ever. He realized that compromise would be necessary and change would come slowly; but as long as the General Assembly moved toward equality by reducing discriminatory practices, he would acquiesce to gradual reform.

But now reform seemed impossible. Radical efforts to extend Republican rule failed when the United States Congress refused to prolong control over Reconstruction in Georgia. White Democrats had been quick to respond. They would control both houses in the next General Assembly. Bullock would likely be impeached and replaced by a conservative governor. Ku Klux activities and other random violence against blacks showed no evidence of subsiding, and the reactionary conservative press continued to stir up resistance to Radical reform. The revolution was going backward.

To Campbell, who would never condone a reversal of the gains to which he had devoted his life, this situation was intolerable. He saw only three courses of action: compromise, emigration (separation), and resistance. The course he selected is evident from his words at the February 1871 Convention of Colored Men in Atlanta. He declared compromise to be out of the question and migration detestable, for to be compelled to move from a rightful home lowered a man's self-esteem and worth. Campbell urged blacks to determine to advance "without compromise" and "in harmony."[69]

He had a flexible mind, and although never changing his goal of equality for all men, he adapted his course to ever-changing conditions. His actions demonstrate that his thinking had progressed from black separatism to negotiation to black power. He had been forced into this transition by whites who would not allow even a limited, initial period of black separatism to work on American soil, by the return to state government of planters with their paternalistic racist ideology, and by his own sense of mission to upgrade his race. Campbell would still attempt reform at the state level from his seat in the legislature, but he determined to concentrate his efforts to force reform at the local level. Through his position as justice of the peace, Campbell turned to black power to neutralize the counterrevolution of white planter resurgence.

CHAPTER THREE

BLACK POWER, WHITE CONSPIRACY

The poisonous Upas has been felled but its roots interlace the soil and will soon send up its destroying twigs.

WILLIAM F. EATON, 1866

The Southern white politician who predicted the failure of Reconstruction left no stone unturned in making his prophecy an accomplished fact. Intrigues, bribery, murder and rapine destroyed the Reconstruction of the Southern States and defeated Republican rule.

DANIEL A. STRAKER, 1893

lthough Campbell still sought to negotiate with Democrats in the state senate, he knew that compromise from a position of political weakness could not advance ailing black social, economic, and political rights. During the long 1871 recess from the General Assembly, Campbell concentrated on the latent power of Darien's black majority to force reform. He had always looked closely after the interests of Darien blacks, but now he increased his efforts on their behalf. He steadfastly determined to end the harsh treatment whites perpetrated on his "children." His efforts increased local black power and militancy; at the same time, they caused whites to accelerate their efforts to depose him. For four years, Campbell successfully resisted.

By 1871 most McIntosh County whites understood that Campbell would tolerate no use of force against blacks. They knew that he legally possessed a strong retaliatory power as justice of the peace, and they were certain he would use that power to enforce equal treatment. Four years of confrontation had taught them lessons white outsiders could not know. Darien was a relatively cosmopolitan town, filled with nonresidents associated with the lumber industry. Robert Penn Warren wrote that after the long journey downstream, a raftsman encountered "at Darien . . . all the excitement of a real city, with foreign masts against the sky and foreign language in his ears."[1] Many upriver and other white outsiders visited the port city, offering opportunities for black-white confrontation. Campbell determined to protect his race from any abuses perpetrated by these transients.

Blacks served as crew members on many of the ships that daily arrived and departed; as many as sixty vessels at once waited to load at Darien or Doboy Island, the main port in McIntosh County. On July 3, 1871, *Grace,* a ship of English registry bound for Le Havre, France, arrived at Doboy. Shortly thereafter, Captain John Irvine placed five of the black crewmen in the Darien jail on a warrant for failure to comply with their contracts. The crewmen maintained that they had signed on in New York to ship only as far as Savannah, but Irvine had compelled them to continue to Doboy and was now holding them until the ship departed for Europe. They complained that Irvine had unjustly detained them and had beaten them with a belaying-pin. They had bruises to prove the mistreatment.[2]

McIntosh's black ordinary, Lewis Jackson, freed the sail-

ors and sent them to Campbell. On July 14, Campbell issued
a warrant for Irvine on the charge of assault and battery
and for using abusive language against citizens of the
United States. He sent constable Hamilton Jackson and five
armed men to Doboy to impound the *Grace,* arrest Irvine,
and bring him to Darien. Campbell instructed the officers
not to allow Irvine to use abusive language against them.
He also levied a bill for $134.68 for wages due the seamen
and $58.60 for court costs. He dismissed the charges Irvine
filed against the seamen and placed the captain on a $26,000
bond.[3]

Irvine protested the charges and the incarceration and secured a local attorney, L. E. B. DeLorme, who went to Savannah and convinced United States Commissioner Henry
Wayne to issue warrants against Campbell and his six "conspirators" for violation of the Ku Klux Act. Court officers
arrested Campbell and his six codefendants and took them
to Savannah. On August 17, Judge George Lee decided that
Campbell "had grievously erred in judgment" but that no
evidence of a conspiracy existed, and therefore Campbell
was not subject to criminal prosecution. Lee dismissed
charges against all seven defendants. Irvine neither pursued the case nor recovered the services of the black seamen.[4]

William M. Sessions, superior court judge of the Brunswick Circuit, mentioned the case in October 1871 in testifying before a congressional subcommittee investigating the
Ku Klux Klan. Judge Sessions came from a lower-middle-
class family of Pike County farmers, who sold or freed their
nine slaves sometime before 1840. He studied law in 1849,
the year of his father's death, and moved to Appling County
in south Georgia. In 1860, at thirty-three years of age, he was
elected to the superior court in Brunswick, a position he held
for thirteen years. In the course of answering questions be-

fore the subcommittee, Judge Sessions upheld Campbell's behavior toward Irvine:

> QUESTION: . . . If the sea captain had enlisted a crew, either black or white, for a certain length of time, at the end of which they were to be discharged, and he were then to attempt by violence or by his authority as master of the vessel, to force them to continue longer on his vessel, would you not regard that as a very great outrage?
>
> ANSWER: I should, certainly.
>
> QUESTION: Can you conceive of a much greater outrage upon a man's private rights?
>
> ANSWER: I could not.
>
> QUESTION: It is practically slavery for the length of time, is it not?
>
> ANSWER: I should think so.
>
> QUESTION: If such a case were presented to a magistrate, would you not think it his duty to interpose and try to relieve these persons?
>
> ANSWER: I should think so.
>
> QUESTION: You certainly would do it?
>
> ANSWER: If those representations were made to me, I should interpose.[5]

Campbell had successfully protected five petitioners from further mistreatment at the hands of an abusive white man. Although his arrest of an English captain, seizure of a foreign ship, and establishment of excessive bail were questionable if not unlawful international acts, the results were commendable, and they enhanced his position among his followers. The case also emboldened Campbell to take further action in support of black rights. Judge Sessions said of Campbell, "He makes up his mind and pursues his course, whether right or wrong. . . . He professes to look, and his acts show that he does look, very closely to their [blacks'] rights as citizens."[6]

The case outraged most whites. One conservative paper, the *Savannah Morning News,* called Campbell a "lawless nigger" who was reveling in his victory and promising his supporters "to do in the future exactly as he had done in the past, and take the consequences." Campbell ignored the slander of the Democrats and resolved to continue his course.[7]

Less than ten days after his quasi-exoneration on the conspiracy charge, Campbell again became embroiled in an international controversy similar to the Irvine case. This time an all-black crew charged English Captain J. Hatfield of the timber ship *Mona* with mistreating them by not properly feeding them. When they refused to obey orders on these grounds, Hatfield shot one of them. When the ship arrived in Darien two days later, the crew "arrested" Hatfield and carried him to Campbell. After a hearing, Campbell jailed the captain for assault and battery with intent to kill. Three days later Hatfield deposited a security bond with a local merchant and gained release from jail. He obtained a new hearing but this time went before the white justice of the peace, J. P. Gilson, who dismissed the case. Hatfield somehow hired a new crew, and the *Mona* departed. He filed for damages, but there is no evidence that anything came from the suit.[8]

On Halloween Campbell testified in Atlanta before the congressional subcommittee investigating Ku Klux activities in Georgia. Campbell spoke of threats made against him but cleverly commented that he did not know whether they came from the Klan: "I called them Ku-Klux, but they are nobody else but the white people." Campbell testified that during his 1868 campaign trip through the Second District, angry whites in Liberty County threatened to "shoot me down on sight," but the large majority of blacks protected him. Only one journey through Tatnall County, which had a white majority, convinced him that "they had too

Black families carving out independent lives on land of their own
(Photo by Rudolf Eickemeyer, Jr.; Special Collections,
University of Georgia Libraries)

General William Tecumseh Sherman
(Georgia Department of Archives
and History)

Contrabands following Sherman's army through Georgia
(*Leslie's Illustrated Newspaper*, March 18, 1865)

General Oliver Otis Howard, commissioner of the Bureau of Refugees, Freedmen, and Abandoned Lands (Photo by George Barnard; Special Collections, University of Georgia Libraries)

Possessory title of forty acres issued to freedman Peter Lloyd (National Archives)

Facing page: On St. Catherines Island, abandoned slave quarters into which freedmen moved in 1865 (William E. Wilson Photographic Archive, Special Collections, University of Georgia Libraries)

Below: Freedmen on St. Catherines Island, late 1870s (William E. Wilson Photographic Archive, Special Collections, University of Georgia Libraries)

A school for the children of freedmen in Liberty County, 1880s
(William E. Wilson Photographic Archive, Special Collections,
University of Georgia Libraries)

"The First Vote"
(*Harper's Illustrated Weekly*,
November 16, 1867)

Discussion of political questions and voting
procedures (*Harper's Illustrated Weekly*,
July 25, 1868)

Two of the many freedmen—sharecroppers and independent
farmers alike—who plowed their land without the aid
of mule or ox (Georgia Historical Society)

Pounding rice from hull (Georgia Department of Archives
and History)

Picking cotton under supervision on St. Catherines Island,
late 1870s (William E. Wilson Photographic Archive,
Special Collections, University of Georgia Libraries)

Working in the timber industry, which in McIntosh County
provided some freedmen with an alternative to agricultural labor
(William E. Wilson Photographic Archive, Special Collections,
University of Georgia Libraries)

Freedmen—most of whom worked as farmers, tenants, sharecroppers, or agricultural laborers—picking cotton and working in their fields (Photo by Rudolph Eickemeyer, Jr.; Special Collections, University of Georgia Libraries)

Henry McNeal Turner
(*Harper's Illustrated Weekly*,
December 12, 1863)

Prayer meeting at one of the many churches established by
freedmen immediately after the war (*Harper's Illustrated Weekly*,
February 2, 1867)

Rufus Brown Bullock, Georgia's only
elected Republican governor,
1868–71 (Special Collections,
University of Georgia Libraries)

Benjamin F. Conley, a Republican
who filled Rufus Bullock's unexpired
term as governor, 1871–72 (Georgia
Department of Archives and History)

James Milton Smith, governor of
Georgia, 1872–77 (Georgia
Department of Archives and History)

Convict laborers in Georgia (Robert E. Williams
Photographic Archive, Special Collections,
University of Georgia Libraries)

many guns for me there." Campbell claimed that during the voter registration process in 1867, someone poisoned him and another registrar. Campbell became very sick, and whites forced him from his bed and compelled him to make a "radical speech." Thinking him exhausted and near death, they allowed him to return to his room, where, to their chagrin, he recovered. According to Campbell, the other victim died a few days later from the effects of the poison.[9]

He told the committee that the latest threat to his life had occurred just two weeks earlier. On October 22, returning from a Convention of Colored People in Columbia, South Carolina, Campbell found his house very quiet and dark. His wife was waiting inside to warn that "there is danger for you; they are determined to kill you before you go to the legislature." Campbell shrugged off this threat as one of many to which he had become accustomed. He accepted the validity of the warning only after several of his friends expressed fears for his safety. Henry Todd, the black owner of one of Darien's sawmills, warned Campbell of the seriousness of the situation. A white man had told him "that Senator will always carry this County as long as he lives . . . he must be got out of the way." As long as he stayed in or around his home, a cordon of black guards who patrolled the grounds protected Campbell. Rumors circulated that when he left for Atlanta to testify, he would be killed. For fear that he might be killed on the steamer from Darien to Savannah, Campbell left the county at night, by horse and buggy.[10]

It is difficult to assess whether this threat was any more serious than the others. Doubtless, whites in general and white leaders in particular wanted to remove him from the county; he was black and powerful, and he stood squarely in the way of the return of white control. Whites fumed over his actions against both local whites and British ship captains, and they blamed him for the difficulties they encoun-

tered with black laborers. They also resented his frequent
trips to Washington to stir up the Radicals against the white
people of Georgia. Additionally, the notoriety his actions
brought to the county embarrassed most whites. No doubt
they viewed his successes as their failures. They wanted to
depose him, but there is little evidence to suggest that they
would have resorted to murder because Campbell's death
might have set off an insurrection. Campbell admitted that
no one had attempted a physical assault because "the rebels
knew that they would be held responsible by the loyal people
of this country, both colored and white, for any injury that
might be done."[11] To get rid of Campbell, the whites had to
persuade the senate to remove him from county office or
prosecute him on real or trumped-up charges and hope for a
conviction and a penitentiary term.

By December 1871, the conservative counterrevolution
surged through Georgia. Democrats returned to their seats
as the majority party in the legislature, thus "redeeming"
the state's political structure. Republican Benjamin Conley
held the governor's chair, but his reign would be short-lived.
Confederate veteran and governor-elect James M. Smith of
Columbus was inaugurated on January 12, 1872, after
being swept into office in a hastily arranged and uncon-
tested election in December. Georgia Democrats, buoyed by
their success, plotted to redeem those local governments still
under "nigger rule."[12]

During the short 1871 session, the legislature had passed
an act establishing a board of commissioners for McIntosh
County. This act empowered the General Assembly to name
seven commissioners who would control matters concerning
county property, taxation, public roads, and elections. The
commissioners had the power to appoint county officers, establish election precincts, collect and disburse county
money, approve of all officers' bonds, and select pilots for the
port of Darien. The act further provided them "with the

same criminal jurisdiction as is now vested in Justices of the Peace," and it stated that "a majority of said commissioners may sit at any time as a Court for County purposes."[13]

The legislature forwarded the act to Governor Conley, who chose to protect Republican interests in McIntosh by pocket-vetoing the measure. He wrote a letter to the infuriated Campbell in which he forecast repassage of the act in January, when the legislature convened under Governor Smith. Less than ten days after the General Assembly met in January, a joint committee met to consider all acts that had expired under Conley; they resolved that the act establishing the commissioners was now law. The next day, January 20, the legislature amended the act, extending to each commissioner the same powers held by justices of the peace and replacing the mayor of Darien with the chairman of the board of commissioners. Campbell was justifiably shaken. Not only did the law provide for an all-white county government with the authority to create and control patronage positions, but it also threatened to destroy Campbell's position. He saw five years of black progress imperiled.[14]

Campbell had been active during the recess before the convening of the new legislature. In Darien, he called several meetings to explain what the return to conservatism would mean to the people of Georgia. He denounced the Democratic state government as racist and corrupt and declared that the bill to establish county commissioners, though temporarily squashed, would soon "abridge their rights and in every way give advantage and supremacy to the whites." He proclaimed the act "the most iniquitous, unjust, and diabolical thing ever attempted on citizens of a free country." He counseled the people to make their desires known and to oppose the implementation of this law. Campbell felt the act was illegal as passed; it properly should have been submitted in a referendum to the voters of McIntosh.[15]

When the legislature convened in January, William Reese

of Washington called the senate's attention to an article in the *Savannah Daily Republican* entitled "Senator Campbell at His Mischief." The article charged Campbell with making inflammatory remarks to his constituents concerning "the oppressive and iniquitous laws . . . [which] completely subjected the negroes to the whites." The piece also stated that Campbell counseled rebellion and had libeled the General Assembly. The writer called for a senate investigation into the matter, which he hoped would "promptly deprive him of his seat."[16]

On January 14, the senate charged its Committee on Privileges and Elections to conduct an investigation and make a recommendation at the fall assembly. Three days later, Senator Rufus E. Lester of Savannah introduced a petition from McIntosh County citizens that charged Campbell with malpractice in office. William Robert Gignilliat had engineered this petition; his letter to Lester indicates his resolve to remove Campbell from McIntosh: "His influence is a blight on the community. If he could be arraigned before the Senate and dismissed for malpractice as a Justice of the Peace, his expulsion from that body would necessarily follow. As he lives only by his office he would then be obliged to quit the County or starve."[17] Lester seized the initiative and joined the conspiracy by presenting the petition to the senate.

The Committee on Privileges and Elections sent a three-man investigating subcommittee to Darien in May 1872. They interviewed and took affidavits from at least forty people who had witnessed Campbell's actions or could attest to his character and motives. Additionally, 129 McIntosh County citizens presented the subcommittee with a petition in support of their senator and rebuking the Lester petition as originating from a small group of "wrongfully and maliciously prejudiced . . . [citizens who] have no just or reasonable grounds to ask for his removal." The petitioners praised Campbell for "using his means and time for the education of the colored people." They explained further that Campbell "is doing all in his power to encourage the colored people to work steady and save their money so that they may buy homes for themselves and children."[18]

All the witnesses for Campbell were blacks; they consistently supported his January speech against the commissioners bill and the effects of his teachings in the county. Clergyman Samuel Ross, the first to testify for Campbell, swore that he encouraged peace between the races and always advised blacks to work hard to provide for themselves and their families. He maintained that Campbell did not counsel resistance to the commissioners themselves but against the bill as being illegal. Campbell had merely presented the case to the people, and "if they agreed to it he would bow to it," but if they opposed it, he would fight for its repeal.[19]

Toby Maxwell told the committee that Campbell had merely sought to learn his constituents' attitudes concerning the commissioners bill. If they wanted a change of rule, he would abide by their wishes. He recalled that Campbell advised blacks to appeal to the courts for redress of grievances and to abide by the law. The other six defense witnesses endorsed Ross's stance and agreed with Maxwell that Campbell's influence was beneficial and his judicial administration fair.[20]

All of the eighteen people who swore in affidavits adverse to Campbell were businessmen, county officials, or both. Two had become county commissioners under the new law; at least two had been jailed by Campbell's court; and one, W. R. Gignilliat, had been Campbell's Democratic opponent and senatorial replacement during the 1868 election and 1870 purge. One-third of the opposition's witnesses were black, but their willingness to testify against Campbell can be explained by their jobs: five held county positions of clerk of the court, sheriff, deputy sheriff, ordinary, and assistant marshal. The board of commissioners controlled their future in these positions. Historian E. Merton Coulter conceded that at least one of them was an "Uncle Tom."[21] Perhaps they all were.

Two of the richest men in the county, William R. Pritchard and Julian Epping, testified that Campbell exerted a "pernicious and wicked influence over the Negroes" and called his January 1872 speech denouncing the commissioners bill "highly inflammatory tending to create estrangement and strife between the races." Both agreed that when Campbell was absent from the county, the black population remained orderly and restrained.[22]

W. A. Burney affirmed these observations, saying that Campbell's speeches stirred up black resistance because of his pronouncements "that certain laws were awful, oppressive, and discriminatory against his race and should not therefore be obeyed." He added that he believed Campbell's speeches demoralized labor and represented "evil."[23]

Perhaps the most damning testimony against Campbell came from his adopted son, E. E. Howard, the clerk of the superior court of McIntosh County. Campbell and Howard's estrangement grew out of an 1870 meeting of blacks in Darien in which Campbell had denounced Howard for his failure surreptitiously to add blacks to the jury rolls. Campbell felt that each individual must judge the merits of each law, and if he found it oppressive, he must resist it and, if necessary, forcibly change it. Obviously Campbell wanted juries to represent the county's population fairly. He understood that for the freedmen to become free men, equal under the law and equal in fact, they must have the right to the same roles as all citizens, including sitting as part of a jury. To be excluded there, of course, enforced in black minds— and in white minds—a distinction which Campbell fought to extinguish. The jury law resembled the commissioners bill in that both deterred black advancement; consequently, both called for resistance. Howard would not disobey even an unjust law, so he and his father grew apart. Howard testified that Campbell's influence among the black population was absolute and that to defy him imperiled one's life and property.[24]

Campbell was indeed willing to employ force to protect black rights. In 1872, his militia formed the core of his political organization. In McIntosh County, blacks outnumbered whites as early as 1793, and in 1872 they held a four-to-one majority. Campbell organized this majority into an effective community. The strength of his organization was undeniable, and he maintained its energy by holding frequent meetings. His ability to bring his people together from the widespread plantations and farms around Darien illustrates the effectiveness of his network. Campbell often tested his followers' responsiveness by calling meetings on the spur of the moment, sometimes in the middle of a work day. Sea Island planter Frances Leigh lamented that whites had no control over their workers, who insisted on "throwing all our authority to the wind, and following Campbell wherever he chose to lead them." Another citizen added that when Campbell called a meeting, word spread through the countryside, and "they invariably, always come."[25]

Although Campbell's political machine possessed both numbers and organization, it lost some control over county offices and officeholders after the legislature passed the commissioners bill. Yet Campbell met this threat by increasing retribution against whites who mistreated blacks. He maintained his power by using the well-proven white tactic of intimidation. His strategy played on old fears of slave insurrection. One prominent Darienite worried that Campbell "could incite the negro population to massacre the whites at any time." White anxieties escalated when blacks carried hunting rifles about the streets, refused to yield sidewalks, resisted addressing whites by titles, and exercised other "freedoms." Frances Leigh noted the constant rumors of an uprising and slaughter. Blacks, Leigh said, "seemed to reach a climax of lawless independence; . . . I never slept without a loaded pistol by my bed." Two witnesses before the senate subcommittee voiced the opinion that Campbell could provoke "bloodshed" at his pleasure. The fear of insurrection, coupled with the knowledge that Campbell would fine or jail those who mistreated blacks, meant black power. Leigh affirmed the influence Campbell had achieved: "In vain I implored him [the white overseer] to be firm, and if he gave an order to stand to it; but the invariable answer was, 'It's no use, Miss B[utler], I should only get myself into trouble, and have the negro sheriff sent over by Campbell to arrest me.' And everyone went on the same principle."[26]

White fears were not unfounded. In June 1871, the white magistrate, J. P. Gilson, had Campbell arrested on a bench warrant from Fulton County. On the day of the hearing three hundred armed blacks filled the courtroom and surrounded the building. Campbell had notified them of the trial by having the black bailiff, Hamilton Jackson, spread the word through the militia organization. Describing the blacks' reaction to Campbell's arraignment, one observer commented that "before Judge Gilson, a large number of Negroes were present acting in a very excited and threatening manner and evincing a demonstration to resist by force of arms his [Campbell's] imprisonment . . . this gathering was called by Campbell and controlled by him." Another white citizen predicted that "if they had put him in jail the niggers would have put the jail in the River." Bowing to his fears and to Campbell's power, Gilson released him.[27]

Campbell's January 1872 speech against the commissioners bill increased white fears. Exhorting his listeners to stand firm against oppressive laws, Campbell proposed to call on President Grant to send the military to protect the rights of free people. If Grant did not comply with that request, Campbell thundered that blacks had "one resource left, which was dear to every freeman's heart and that was the musket and Bayonet." He believed that by constant resistance, the people could force the repeal of unjust laws. He liked to use the fugitive slave law as the example of an iniquitous law that people fought to overturn. His background as an idealist, a preacher, and a prewar abolitionist suggests that his exhortations pointed to a higher authority; his remonstrances contain much of abolitionist "higher law" doctrine. He counseled individual resistance, but he spoke in a community context—individual resistance multiplied would produce a combined effort that would stop discrimination and overturn unjust laws.[28]

By following Campbell's counsel, the black majority stalemated the board of commissioners for a time. As late as 1873, S. C. Williams, investigating "difficulties" in Darien, reported to Governor Smith that McIntosh blacks were resisting the commissioners, whom they believed had been illegally appointed. Such widespread resistance rendered "the Board . . . unable to act in its official capacity as it had not the means of enforcing municipal and County ordinances."[29]

While the subcommittee studied the evidence and debated what to recommend to the senate, W. R. Gignilliat, who had sent the petition to Senator Lester asking for the removal of Campbell, helped dredge up a year-old case with which to prosecute him. This was part of the dual effort to remove Campbell from his offices. The Redeemers hoped the senate investigation would strip Campbell of his political position; then they would throw him in prison to remove him from the county. During the April 1872 term of the McIntosh County Superior Court, a grand jury indicted Campbell for the false imprisonment of a white citizen on February 4, 1871.[30]

The events that led to the purported false imprisonment began the day after Campbell returned to Darien from the

Atlanta Convention of Colored Men. John M. Fisher came before him to swear out an arrest warrant for two blacks he accused of burglarizing his bakery. Campbell issued a warrant and commanded a constable to execute it. The constable assembled a posse to hunt for the offenders but failed to find or arrest anyone. The posse did recover much of the stolen property. When Campbell presented Fisher with a $73 bill for costs, Fisher balked and, after consulting with his attorney, W. R. Gignilliat, refused to pay. When Campbell warned Fisher that the penalty for not paying was imprisonment, Fisher compounded his contempt by adamantly refusing, telling Campbell he had no right to charge such exorbitant fees for costs. Campbell recalled that Fisher contended "that he had no business to respect a court held by a negro." Campbell cited the following exchange: "I said, 'Mr. Fisher, I hope you will not say anything more.' He said, 'I will say it and will not pay it; you have no business to charge it.' I said, 'Mr. Fisher, if you don't cease this I will hold you for contempt.' He said, 'I don't care.' I then had him arrested for contempt."[31]

Campbell sentenced Fisher to five hours in jail, but on the advice of Gignilliat, who saw an opportunity to remove Campbell from office, Fisher remained in jail for two or three days. Campbell remembered that Gignilliat told Fisher to stay in jail so he could "fix" Campbell. Judge Sessions heard the case on a writ of habeas corpus and released Fisher but declined to issue a warrant against Campbell for false imprisonment. Sessions advised Fisher that he could get the white magistrate, J. P. Gilson, to issue a warrant for Campbell, but Gilson refused, saying he could not get such a warrant obeyed. The case seemingly died.[32]

But now that the Democrats were making a concerted effort to remove blacks from office and influence, they exhumed this case as their best hope to oust Campbell. A trial at this time could only hurt Campbell with the senate investigating team. The Redeemers rejoiced at the turn of events and hoped that one of their tactics would remove Campbell from state and county offices and the other would put him in a chain gang in some spot remote from Darien.

During the April 1872 term of the McIntosh County Superior Court, a jury found Campbell guilty of the false imprisonment of John Fisher. Campbell raised questions about the procedure used to select the jurors as well as the judge's charge to that jury. Apparently, Judge William Schley had wrongly allowed the exclusion of ten jurors and had further prejudiced the case by mistakenly quoting the law to the jury: "If you find from the testimony and the warrant that it [the imprisonment of Fisher] was manifestly illegal the law presumes malice."[33]

While Campbell's lawyers appealed his case to the Georgia Supreme Court, he went free on bail. The Redeemers continued their efforts to keep him occupied with lawsuits. In late June, a Fulton County court issued a warrant for Campbell that charged him with violating Georgia law by marrying a black man and a white woman in Atlanta in 1868. Officers arrested Campbell in Savannah, which they could not have done in Darien without chancing a riot, and put him in jail for three days before taking him to Atlanta. After spending another four days in an Atlanta jail, Campbell was tried and released. The judge called the affair a "broad farce." Campbell contended that the marriage had taken place in a public house at 10:30 at night and he had been under the impression the woman was a "bright mulatto."[34]

The prosecutor of the case is unknown, but it is safe to assume that this incident was another Redeemer attempt to keep Campbell out of McIntosh County and embroiled in legal battles. Black leader Henry McNeal Turner of Macon wrote a letter to the editor of the *Savannah Journal* insisting that there was a statewide conspiracy to send black lead-

ers to jail. He cited Campbell's case as the prime example of
Democratic action: "Last Tuesday Senator Campbell was arrested and incarcerated in jail. The senator is handcuffed as
though he was a murderous desperado and hurried off to
Atlanta. And what is all this for? Why manacle, shackle,
and gyve this senator with such unusual ferocity? Is it because he married that couple four years ago? No! It is because they mean to get him out of the senate and defeat his
re-election." Campbell knew that his troubles stemmed from
his Radical politics.[35]

But Campbell refused to be intimidated by threats to
change his course. When the senate met in July, he was in
his seat promoting black interests. His 1872 senate record is
admirable, especially considering the trying conditions he
faced that year. He proposed a bill to force planters and
businessmen to redeem scrip they had issued to their employees during the postwar money shortage. Now that
money was available, they were increasing profits by refusing to make good the outstanding scrip. The senate voted
the bill down.[36]

Campbell continued his campaign to upgrade education
for all children, regardless of race. He wanted to stop discrimination in public schools. On August 9 he asked the senate to strike all legal provisions that prevented the integra-
tion of Georgia schools. Specifically, he moved to strike the
words "provided that colored and white children should not
attend the same school." He lost both attempts. The 1872
law did provide for equal school facilities as far as practi-
cable but insisted that the races "shall not be taught" in
common classrooms.[37] Campbell's only success in educational reform came when the senate approved his motion to
appropriate one-third of the receipts of the agricultural land
scrip to an all-black college. Atlanta University, chartered
in 1867, formally opened in 1869. It graduated its first class
in 1876 and today incorporates Morehouse, Spelman, Clark,

and Morris Brown colleges in one facility. North Georgia College at Dahlonega and the college at Milledgeville would also receive one-third each. The 1862 Morrill Land Grant Act provided each state with western lands that could be sold to obtain money for establishing agricultural and mechanical schools. In 1872, Georgia sold the land scrip for $243,000. But on orders from Governor Smith, all the receipts went to support white students at the University of Georgia. Campbell had won only a paper victory.[38]

Two days before the end of the session, August 23, 1872, the Committee on Privileges reported to the senate on Campbell's alleged misconduct. The committee found Campbell "guilty of using disrespectful and slanderous language towards the Senate . . . guilty of trying to excite an insurrectionary spirit among the people of his district by advising them to resist a public law of the State with the bayonet," guilty of being "a general disturber of the peace and order . . . [and] guilty of malpractice in the office of Justice of the Peace." The committee satisfied itself that the evidence against Campbell was valid but declined to make a recommendation for senate action. Equally strange, the senate chose not to pursue Campbell's removal at that time. Perhaps the senators feared that his expulsion would send him on another trip to Washington and lead to reinstitution of military Reconstruction. Whatever the reason, Campbell's influence soared among his followers when the senate failed to oust him. He had counseled the blacks to resist with the bayonet if necessary, and he still sat in the senate.[39]

Campbell returned to Darien to campaign for his senate seat and to support the reelection of Grant for president and David Walker for governor. The *Savannah Morning News* reported that because of that "monkey-faced evil spirit, Tunis G. Campbell and his ready vassalmen," McIntosh County was "one of the strongholds of Radicalism and Grantism in Georgia."[40]

While campaigning, Campbell continued to look after black rights. On the night of September 9, the steamer *Nick King,* stopped in Darien on its regularly scheduled route between Savannah and Jacksonville, embarked passengers and freight. A black stevedore, Godfrey Jackson, was busily loading baggage when he accidentally backed into the ship's captain. Captain Nick King grabbed him with both hands and threw him under the trunk he had been loading. Later, Jackson complained to Campbell, and on the ship's return trip through Darien, Campbell had King arrested and put under a $300 bond to appear at the next superior court. Back in July, Campbell had written U.S. Senator E. D. Morgan, chairman of the Republican National Committee, that "in McIntosh County there is better protection to Life & Property than in any other County in Georgia." He intended to uphold that statement.[41]

In the 1872 election, Campbell faced H. W. Mattox of Liberty County for the Second District senate seat. The election on October 2 yielded the results shown in Table 4. Although Campbell had successfully reclaimed his seat, the numbers for Tatnall County suggest fraud in the race for governor. Tatnall County's vote for governor most likely split in accord with the senate race, as did those in McIntosh and Liberty.

TABLE 4. ELECTION RESULTS, 1872

	Governor		Senate	
	Smith	Walker	Mattox	Campbell
McIntosh	109	563	109	557
Liberty	367	595	355	607
Tatnall	891	0	652	217
Totals	1,377	1,158	1,116	1,381

Source: "T. G. Campbell vs. H. W. Mattox," Contested Elections, Second District, 1872, GDAH.

The irregularity carried the Second District for Smith but made little difference in the statewide tally.

Officials in Liberty County, however, "discovered" irregularities in two precincts. Polls at the Hinesville courthouse had remained open two hours past the six o'clock closing time provided by law, even though candidate Mattox, County Judge William Norman, and the sheriff had personally supervised the voting. The sheriff was supposed to ensure proper closing. At another polling place in the county, Riceboro, the election managers had signed themselves "JP" and "FH" instead of writing out "Justice of the Peace" or "Freeholder." Liberty officials declared both sets of returns invalid and changed the consolidated return results as follows:

Smith	Walker	Mattox	Campbell
213	0	210	5

This changed the total District returns:

Smith	Walker	Mattox	Campbell
1,213	563	971	779

Campbell immediately contested the election on the grounds that Liberty County had illegally thrown out the votes of two precincts. On January 14, 1873, Campbell's challenge reached the General Assembly. While the Committee on Privileges and Elections debated the matter, Mattox took his seat.[42]

Meanwhile, the Georgia high court reversed the decision of the McIntosh County Superior Court. The court found that the jury had been irregularly drawn and was thereby unfairly biased against Campbell. The supreme court also found Judge Schley's charge to the jury in error because "the law does not presume malice against a judicial officer because he renders an illegal judgment."[43] Campbell had eluded criminal charges; he did not escape Redeemer wrath in the senate.

On January 22, 1874, the senate Committee on Privileges and Elections recommended that Mattox be given his seat on the grounds that Campbell had not legally given him notice that he had contested the election. Not only had the committee procrastinated about Campbell's protest for 374 days—an obvious scheme to prevent him from being seated —but it claimed proper notice had not been given. Campbell had, in fact, contested the election as early as November 1872. By a vote of thirty-seven to two, the senate declared Mattox the winner. Election fraud and committee misdealings ousted Campbell from his seat. Instead of recontesting, Campbell concentrated on improving conditions in and around Darien.[44]

Even though the superior court had acted incorrectly and therefore did not give Campbell a fair trial, the question remains: had Campbell been guilty of falsely imprisoning Fisher for contempt? Testifying before the Ku Klux Committee in November 1871, Judge Sessions of the McIntosh County Superior Court defined contempt as "any disorder; for instance, using disrespectful language to the court or anything of that sort." He agreed that any language scornful of the authority of the court would be considered contempt and that the presiding magistrate had to decide personally what actions constituted contempt in each case. Sessions believed that even if an officer acted wrongly but in good faith, no grounds existed for charging him with false imprisonment. Perhaps in the Fisher case Campbell had been overly sensitive about his authority and had acted hastily, but he clearly had acted in good faith in trying to uphold the dignity of his court.[45]

During 1873 and 1874, Campbell oversaw labor and social relations in McIntosh County. No incidents of abuses on the waterfront at Darien or Doboy were reported. Apparently, sea captains and others had learned that if they expected to profit from the timber trade near Darien, they must not abuse blacks. Campbell encouraged this tranquillity by swift retaliatory action and by stationing armed men in the street at various times. He controlled the only organized militia force in the county, which, by 1874, Fortune Ross and Nero West had drilled for more than three years.[46]

But this relative calm did not mean that the Democrats had ceased their effort to be rid of "the Gubner of the Hottentots" and thereby redeem the county. One McIntosh County diarist recorded that there remained a "bad state of feeling between whites and blacks in Darien." In June 1873, white Justice of the Peace Theodore P. Pease, a Darien merchant with $29,235 worth of property, issued a warrant charging Campbell with holding two pistols belonging to R. E. Carr. The sheriff arrested Campbell, but a mob of blacks prevented further action. Then in December 1873, Isaac Rafe charged Campbell with falsely imprisoning him after he failed to raise bail, but the case did not reach the court until 1875.[47]

By this time, the Republican party had split into two factions: a moderate wing led by John E. Bryant of Augusta and a Radical wing led by Campbell and others who refused to compromise with the Redeemers. Both groups actively campaigned in the 1874 state and congressional elections. In May the moderates nominated Bryant for the U.S. Congress from the First District, which included McIntosh County. Campbell threw his support to a Radical Bolter, Jesse Wimberly of Savannah, who worked as a clerk in the Savannah Customs Office and owned a small farm in adjoining Burke County. Little is known of his platform except that it urged blacks to stand together against the Democrats and the moderate Republicans.[48]

During the campaign, Campbell often stood at Wimberly's side, introducing him at political meetings, making

speeches supporting his election, and everywhere denouncing Bryant as a white mercenary who had sold out black
interests to the Democrats. At least three times, Campbell
shared a platform with Bryant at political rallies in Darien.
On the first occasion, a reporter for the *Darien Timber Gazette* wrote that blacks pledged themselves to support "the
great Tycoon of McIntosh . . . to the end." Of the second
meeting, the reporter noted that when Bryant supporters
accused Campbell of abuses, "angry expressions and movements in the crowd indicated unmistakenly how the feeling
lay." The crowd threatened action, but Campbell quieted
them and easily won the encounter. At the third meeting,
when Bryant slandered Campbell, the crowd "made a rush
for the stand and smashed it into a hundred pieces." Bryant
escaped the county with a mob at his heels. Not only had
Campbell united the blacks; he had so completely won their
affections that they would not allow a white man, even a
Republican, to speak against him. In the election, Wimberly
easily beat Bryant in McIntosh, 394 to 68.[49]

Bryant's votes resulted from a split among blacks over the
McIntosh County seat in the Georgia House of Representatives. Late in the campaign, Campbell had decided not to
run for his senate seat, probably feeling that he could not
win in the face of probable election fraud in Tatnall and Liberty counties. Instead, he announced for the house. This decision miffed some of his former supporters who had already
decided to support black sheriff James Bennett for that office. At the county convention, delegates nominated Bennett
and another man for the post, but both withdrew upon real-
izing that Campbell enjoyed overwhelming support. Bennett
then ran an independent campaign, and the *Darien Timber
Gazette* gave him quasi-support in hopes that this breach
would elect the Democrat A. S. Barnwell. The newspaper
printed an appeal from Lectured Crawford, who claimed to
have lost confidence in Campbell as a party leader. Craw-

ford had political designs of his own but temporarily supported Bennett. Ironically, Campbell had succeeded so well in involving blacks in politics, or at least in making them politically aware, that some few now opposed his election. These members of the black bourgeoisie owed their positions to their own pluck and to Campbell but feared for their offices after passage of the commissioners bill. Hoping to maintain their newly acquired status, and no doubt fully aware of the increasing Democratic pressure to remove Campbell, they sought to accommodate whites. But Campbell remained the voters' choice. The vote was Campbell, 481; Bennett, 77; and Barnwell, 282. White election managers declared 174 votes illegal—155 of them Campbell's—but he still won by 60 votes. Barnwell contested the election, but his appeal had to wait until the legislature convened in January.[50]

Campbell seemed secure atop his powerful black political machine. He had met Bennett's challenge with a six-to-one majority. A few nights after the election, fire swept through Darien's business section. Bennett's merchandise store with its shelves stocked with goods was destroyed, and John Fisher's bakery burned to the ground. Whether Campbell's supporters started the fire is unknown, but the blaze seemed to be an obvious statement: opposition to Campbell invited retaliation, either from an act of God or of man.[51]

In January 1875, the McIntosh County Superior Court met in Darien under a new judge. Governor Smith had appointed Henry B. Tompkins of Savannah to fill the vacancy created by the resignation of Judge Schley. Tompkins, a thirty-year-old bachelor, a staunch Democrat, and a Confederate veteran, insisted on setting Darien "to rights." McIntosh blacks noted his obvious "animosity against the colored people" and his desire to send Campbell to the penitentiary. His appointment proved to be part of the conspiracy black leader Henry M. Turner reported in 1872: "Soon after Governor Smith went into the Executive chair, the Negro-haters concluded to change their tactics and the threat went abroad that Negro leaders must go to the penitentiary."[52]

On January 9, the grand jury indicted Campbell for the false imprisonment of Isaac Rafe. In 1873 Campbell had arrested Rafe and charged him with breaking into two houses owned by blacks and with abusive behavior. Campbell fined Rafe $100 and instructed him to keep the peace for six months. On the advice of bondsman Walter A. Ray, Rafe refused to pay court costs or bond. Campbell then ordered Rafe to jail, but according to Campbell, Rafe ran away and never spent one minute behind bars. The prosecutor in this case, the same Walter A. Ray, produced an affidavit signed by himself which stated that Rafe had paid the bond. Campbell denied that claim.[53]

Questions arose over the process of selecting the jury for Campbell's trial. Campbell and his attorneys challenged the procedure, believing the list of prospective jurors had been rigged to ensure a hostile jury. Of the forty-eight jurors called, all had answered present. At least two of the eleven whites selected had had confrontations with Campbell in the past, and the lone black juror was Lectured Crawford, the moderate who had denounced Campbell in the last election. In the county, blacks outnumbered white voters three to one; the jury did not represent these statistics.[54]

Yet even with this hostile jury, the flimsy evidence and fears of black retaliation produced no decision by ten o'clock on the night of the trial. Tompkins brought the jury men before him and threatened to recess from midnight until the middle of the next week, promising to sequester them until then unless they reached a decision soon. Within fifteen minutes, the jury found Campbell guilty as charged but recommended mercy. Campbell's counsel did not appeal the conviction, later saying that "under the recommendation of mercy by the jury, [I thought the judge] would simply fine

Mr. Campbell a moderate sum, and imprison him in the common jail" for a short period. Tompkins, however, disregarded the recommendation for mercy. He stripped Campbell of his office as justice of the peace and sentenced him "to be taken *at once* by the Sheriff of McIntosh County to the common jail of Chatham County (there being no secure jail in McIntosh County) and . . . thence to be taken to the Penitentiary . . . to be confined at hard labor for . . . One (1) year."[55]

On hearing the sentence, Campbell's attorneys, I. W. Christian of Darien and Martin Menshon of Brunswick, approached the bench to appeal for bond. Tompkins gruffly refused, saying that he "would not take a bond for the sum of a million dollars." Menshon then moved for a new trial, but Tompkins declared the court adjourned and set a hearing on the motion for the following week in Savannah. At the appointed day and time Menshon appeared in Savannah, but Tompkins put off the hearing each day until a guard from the state penitentiary came and took Campbell away.[56]

Tompkins knew he could not hold Campbell in Darien, so he had ordered him to Savannah immediately after the trial. This tactic caught Campbell's supporters off guard, and they did not respond. Instead, a mob of supporters followed Campbell for a while before turning back to Darien in despair. Whites jubilantly celebrated. One wrote the *Timber Gazette:* "We want no other Judge than Henry B. Tompkins."[57]

The penitentiary guard took Campbell by train to Milledgeville for three or four days until he was reassigned to the convict labor camp in the Dade County coal mines, Georgia's largest lessee of prisoners. During his journey to Dade County, Campbell spent a night in the Atlanta jail. An old acquaintance, Romulus Moore, hired two lawyers to represent him. They secured a writ of habeas corpus from the Fulton County ordinary.[58]

The *Atlanta Constitution* reported that when Campbell

was brought before the county ordinary, Judge Daniel Pitt-man, "the courtroom was densely packed with negroes, all of whom were friends of the prisoner. Among them we noticed nearly all of the prominent colored men in this com-munity." Campbell's attorneys, W. F. Wright and D. P. Hill, asked for a postponement to obtain evidence from Savannah that would show that Campbell had been allowed neither bond nor the right to appeal to a higher court. Pittman over-ruled the motion. Wright then presented a petition stating that Campbell could not get a fair trial in Georgia courts and requested a change of venue to the U.S. Circuit Court. Pittman also overruled that motion.[59]

While Campbell's lawyers appealed to an Atlanta superior court, Pittman ordered Campbell to a nearby prison camp, where he labored for two days. Superior Court Judge John L. Hopkins issued a writ of habeas corpus and brought Campbell before him. At the hearing, Hopkins concluded that Campbell was entitled to be released on bail while at-torneys appealed his case to the Georgia Supreme Court. Be-cause the committing judge had the right to set bail, Hop-kins applied to Tompkins to set bail and ordered the McIntosh County ordinary to accept out-of-county bonds. Tompkins delayed responding to the request and initially re-fused to turn over papers necessary to allow bail. After much delay, while Campbell's wife tried to get the proper papers, Tompkins finally relented and released Campbell on a $2000 bond. His release notwithstanding, white Demo-crats celebrated the turn of events. On January 23, the *Tim-ber Gazette* quoted the Atlanta correspondent to the *Savan-nah Advertiser:* "Everybody at the capitol is jubilant over the initial exploits of your new Judge in the administration of criminal law in the negro bestridden County of McIntosh. He has rid the County of . . . the Senior Campbell. His pres-ence here is as little welcome as it is on the coast and there is a general rejoicing among the members over the prospects of filling his seat with a better man."[60]

In the interim, the Georgia General Assembly had reconvened, and the Committee on Petitions and Elections considered A. S. Barnwell's claim to Campbell's seat. Barnwell argued that one of the election managers, E. M. Blount, was not a freeholder as the law required, thus invalidating every vote cast under his supervision. Barnwell was correct—Blount owned no land. The Board of Commissioners had appointed the election managers, and it is difficult to imagine that they did not know that Blount, a white man and long-time resident of the county, did not own land. It is more likely that Blount's appointment was part of the conspiracy to remove Campbell from power. It worked. The House of Representatives seized the chance to depose Campbell and voted to seat Barnwell in his stead.[61]

After his release on bail, Campbell immediately applied for his seat in the legislature. Glynn County representative Jim Blue read Campbell's petition claiming the right to his seat, but the house stood by its decision to throw out the votes from the Darien precinct and declared Barnwell the winner by eleven votes.[62]

Campbell had nothing left to do in Atlanta, so he decided to return to Darien and continue to resist Redeemer rule. He never reached Darien, for upon his arrival in Savannah in March, Tompkins arrested him on a bench warrant and put him in the Chatham County jail. The charge was false imprisonment of John Fisher, the same case reversed by the Georgia Supreme Court in 1873. Tompkins obviously dedicated himself to putting Campbell in the penitentiary or at least tying him up in lengthy court battles to minimize his influence over McIntosh County blacks.[63]

During the February term of the McIntosh County Superior Court, Tompkins declared the 1872 Fisher indictment

nolle-prossed (canceled); he then presented a new indictment against Campbell. Assistant U.S. Attorney George S.
Thomas wrote to U.S. Attorney General Edwards Pierrepont
insisting that Tompkins was persecuting Campbell because
of his race. Thomas found that the first indictment sup-
posedly had been nolle-prossed for being in incorrect legal
form whereas actually it was done only to keep the four-year
statute of limitations from expiring. In January 1873,
Darien's courthouse fire destroyed all records of the first bill.
Tompkins took advantage of this loss to claim that the indictment had been nolle-prossed for a technicality.[64]

On April 30, 1875, the grand jury of McIntosh County Superior Court indicted Campbell for malpractice in office for
the false imprisonment of Fisher. Tompkins held a hearing
and ordered the county ordinary to accept a valid $3000
bond if Campbell could obtain it. Campbell could not make
bail. Tompkins ordered the sheriff to take him to jail.[65]

Back in January, when Tompkins convicted Campbell in
the Rafe case and quickly took him to Savannah, blacks had
taken no action to prevent his removal. This time they were
ready. When Campbell failed to give bond, the sheriff and
six to eight men attempted to take him to jail. Outside, hundreds of armed blacks, men and women, surrounded the
courthouse and demanded Campbell's release. Tompkins attempted to impose his authority. With four others, he barred
the door of the courthouse while the white city marshal, R. E.
Carr, waded into the crowd to disperse it. Someone knocked
the marshal down and a scuffle ensued; both sides would later
claim that the other fired first. The *Timber Gazette* reported
that after being struck, Carr drew his pistol and fired into the
crowd. The blacks reacted with fifteen or twenty shots, all
aimed at the men clustered in the doorway of the courthouse.
No one was killed, but every officer except Tompkins suffered
wounds. Suddenly the critical moment passed and the crowd
quieted.[66]

With considerable difficulty, Tompkins persuaded twenty men to keep Campbell in the courthouse through the night and prevent his people from freeing him. All night, sporadic shooting rang throughout the town. Blacks looted houses looking for guns, but they made no attempt to fight the posse. By the next evening, both sides remained in position, but no more violence had occurred. Tompkins decided not to risk taking Campbell overland to Savannah. That night, when the northbound steamer *Lizzie Baker* reached Darien, Tompkins and the posse took Campbell through the crowd and aboard the steamer. Campbell apparently made no attempt to incite the blacks to free him. He probably feared for his own safety as well as theirs. As the *Lizzie Baker* pulled away from Darien a large crowd of blacks mournfully chanted, "Goodbye Mas Jesus, goodbye."[67]

Over the next eight months, Campbell twice offered bail, but Tompkins rejected these offers. Campbell and his wife wrote letters to President Grant asking him for relief from the iniquities of conspiring Democrats. In McIntosh County, 263 black males sent a petition to the president begging for relief from the oppressive board of commissioners and from other Democrats who were sending black leaders to the penitentiary and jailing blacks simply because they voted Republican. The petitioners asked Grant to furnish them with guns so they could protect themselves.[68]

By August 10, Tompkins's actions again led the petitioners to apply to Grant for relief. They accused Tompkins of jailing blacks merely for being friends of Campbell and claimed that even women with babies and those over the age of eighty could not escape his wrath. In all, 326 men and 189 women signed the petition asking Grant to send troops to protect them or to send them boxes of rifles so that they might protect themselves. Governor Smith had formed two white militia companies and supplied them with arms to keep the blacks in line. Without their leader or sufficient weapons to confront a well-armed militia, Darien blacks could not resort to force to protect their interests.[69]

C. B. Clark, owner of a large hardware manufactory in Buffalo, New York, had been aboard the *Lizzie Baker* when Tompkins took Campbell to Savannah. Stirred by Campbell's plight, he wrote President Grant asking him to intercede. Grant passed the letter to Attorney General Pierrepont, who ordered the U.S. attorney for Georgia, Henry P. Farrow, to investigate the matter. Assistant U.S. Attorney George S. Thomas took charge of the investigation.[70]

After investigating charges in the Rafe and Fisher cases, Thomas declared Tompkins guilty of persecuting Campbell and unworthy of holding judicial office. He charged Tompkins with setting an unreasonable bail and then refusing to accept valid bonds when Campbell offered them. He interviewed all the attorneys associated with Campbell's cases, one of whom told him that Tompkins had refused bail, saying he "would rather have a bond for his non-appearance than for his appearance." Another Savannah attorney, Elias Yulee, confidently remarked that if Campbell would promise to leave Georgia, Tompkins would release him. After talking with one of Savannah's conservative judges, Thomas wrote Pierrepont:

> Judge Russell very frankly told me that he was a Democrat and opposed to Campbell politically, but that candor compelled him to state that he (Campbell) was being shamefully persecuted by Judge Tompkins and others for the purpose of ridding McIntosh County of his presence and influence . . . and that he was satisfied that Judge Tompkins' prejudices against Mr. Campbell on account of his race and color were such as to disqualify him from giving Mr. Campbell justice, and that he looked upon Judge Tompkins conduct towards Mr. Campbell as a disgrace to the judicial position he occupied.

Two other attorneys and "a number of other persons white and colored" attested to the truth of Russell's observations. They asserted that Tompkins had removed Campbell because of his Radical politics.[71]

Thomas and Farrow worked to transfer Campbell's case to a federal court because of state court prejudice against him. Farrow even considered going to Darien to defend Campbell himself when the Fisher case came to trial. He wrote Pierrepont that Campbell's case was not an isolated one, and "it is difficult for people who do not reside in this country . . . to realize how negroes can be murdered [or jailed] here with such impunity." From July to December, Thomas and Farrow worked to remove the Fisher case to a federal court. Had they succeeded, they would have been both prosecutors and defense attorneys, and Campbell would have gone free.[72]

But time ran out. The Georgia Supreme Court dismissed without a hearing the motion of Campbell's attorneys that there had been jury box tampering in the Rafe case. Citing a discrepancy in Judge Tompkins's certification to the bill of exceptions, the high court ruled that this technical error made the hearing impossible. The case returned to Tompkins's court. The U.S. attorneys had concentrated their efforts on changing the venue of the Fisher case and paid little attention to the Rafe case. Now, because of the supreme court decision, Judge John Erskine of the U.S. Circuit Court in Savannah released the government's claim to Campbell. The next day, January 9, 1876, Tompkins ordered Campbell to be taken at the earliest opportunity from the Chatham County jail, where he had been incarcerated for 256 days, and thence transported to the penitentiary.[73]

Instead of going to the state penitentiary, Campbell, now sixty-three years old, found himself leased out under Georgia's convict-lease law. Campbell described his first day on the gang: "On or about the 12th of January, 1876, the guard

from the State prison came, about 7 o'clock a.m., and handcuffed me, and, with a chain about twelve feet long, dragged
me along the streets of Savannah to the Central railroad,
and then took me one hundred and forty miles from Savannah, to a prison camp on the plantation of Colonel Jack
Smith's, in Washington County, State of Georgia. The
weather was very cold, and they took me up in a wagon. I
was helpless when we got there, at 1 o'clock in the night—
my hands being chained together." Heavily ironed, dressed
in prison clothes, he joined 119 other convicts at work clear-
ing land on T. J. Smith's plantation. For one year, Smith paid
the state $8.25 to hire Campbell and $1,154.06 total for all
the prisoners. Perhaps believing Campbell to be "the Lion of
the Georgia Penitentiary," Smith initially kept him under
heavy guard, but he soon warmed to Campbell's charm, re-
leasing him from irons and hard labor. Smith put Campbell
in charge of his wheelwright and blacksmith shops, fed him
from his own table, and allowed him to preach three times a
week to the other convicts. Campbell remembered Smith as
being very kind to him, but he also said that during his time
there four blacks died from whippings and most of the others had been cruelly treated. Trying to depict the working
conditions, Campbell wrote: "It is impossible to describe the
way in which the prisoners were worked. They were taken
out as soon as they could see—both summer and winter—
and kept to work as long as it was light, with one hour for
dinner. They had breakfast before daylight. If wood was to
be cut, the strongest and most expert men with the ax were
made leaders; and every man had to keep stroke with him
all day long; and if they failed to do so, they were beaten
most unmercifully with a leather strop, or a buggy trace,
and given from fifty to one hundred strokes, until they
would keep up or die."[74]

Campbell's friends attempted to get him released early.
On May 5, 1876, seventeen prominent black citizens from

throughout the state petitioned Governor Smith to pardon Campbell for reasons of age, time already served, and humiliation. Several former legislators, ministers, and newspaper editors were among the signers, including Henry Turner, James M. Simms, J. H. Deveaux, and George Wallace. Predictably, Governor Smith refused their pleas.[75]

On January 6, 1877, T. J. Smith released Campbell from his work camp. The editor of the *Timber Gazette* predicted, "We think it very doubtful if the old man ever comes back to Darien to live anymore." Probably convinced that Tompkins would reincarcerate him and no doubt tired of being jailed, Campbell did not return to McIntosh County. He moved to Washington, D.C., where he tried to develop sympathy and get help for Georgia blacks. In one speech he called Georgia "the Empire State of Rascality" and said that "the colored people of Georgia were today in the hands of their enemies, to do with them as they chose. . . . They have no protection whatever." He also argued his case before President Rutherford B. Hayes; but Hayes was a compromise president in the White House only because of his agreement formally to end Reconstruction, and nothing came of the meeting.[76]

McIntosh County blacks had lost their leader, and Georgia blacks had lost their main legislative proponent. It had taken Democrats eleven years to put Campbell in the penitentiary and thus scare him out of the state. During that time, McIntosh County had been a center of Georgia Radicalism. Campbell's use of black power with its "threatening" meetings, armed militia, and ballot control forestalled Redeemer rule there. But he was finally deposed by a statewide Democratic conspiracy at the highest levels of government. Radical strength at the local level proved insufficient to stop Redeemer power at the state level. While courts, newspapers, and politicians looked the other way, obvious election frauds, political deceptions, jury-tampering, judicial misdealings, and unrelenting persecution by a racist judge put planters back in control in the county and throughout the state. Campbell was gone. But his experiment in self-determination through black power moved McIntosh blacks along the road to becoming free-in-fact. The power of his organization continued to influence Darien's social, economic, and political race relations for years to come.

EPILOGUE

C ampbell's vision for uplifting the black race remained steadfast, even though his tactics shifted from black separatism to negotiation to black power. I have emphasized Campbell's radicalism, and it was radical in that he strove to raise blacks to equality with whites. Yet his vision fit entirely within the mainstream American movement toward bourgeois capitalism. Campbell wanted blacks to experience democracy as equal participants in the American Dream. He tried to make the former chattels into citizens-in-fact, not just citizens-by-law.

A Jeffersonian, Campbell believed in the people, the Declaration of Independence, and education. He wanted a literate, informed citizenry to participate actively in a true democracy. Further, he tied political involvement and property-holding to republicanism. Campbell's ideal nation consisted of self-sufficient small farmers who worked hard, saved their money, educated their children, went to church, made and obeyed just laws, and contributed taxes for the good of all the people. He also, not unlike Jefferson, held in reserve the power of the people to resist unjust laws by nullification or, if necessary, by revolution. And, of course, in Campbell's America, democracy was color blind. It is little wonder that his vision clashed with the entrenched planter racism and way of life. His program for equality was revolutionary in a plantation society long underpinned by stratification of peoples into

caste and class. Campbell confronted the reactionary white
aristocracy with demands that they treat their former property, their slaves, with respect. A flexible thinker, Campbell
adjusted his actions while always striving toward a goal of
equality.

In South Carolina in 1863, Campbell participated in the
Port Royal experiment and learned much from that experience. After the creation of Sherman's reservation on January 16, 1865, Campbell found duty as a Freedmen's Bureau
agent on St. Catherines Island, Georgia. There he instituted
an experiment in black separatism based on the belief that
freedmen could advance faster to becoming free men if they
were shielded from injurious confrontations with unprincipled and exploitive northern or southern whites. His experiment was succeeding, but when President Johnson restored land to the former owners, federal troops forced
Campbell to relocate.

At BelleVille in McIntosh County, Campbell reinstituted
an autonomous black colony, but after Radicals took charge
of Reconstruction, he perceived the opportunity to help
blacks toward equal treatment and material gains. Campbell worked hard to ensure that when Democrats confronted
Republicans over issues important to blacks, Radicals would
be negotiating from a position of political strength. He registered voters, helped draft the Georgia constitution, represented Second District voters in the state senate, sat on the
state Republican Central Committee, influenced the passage of the Ku Klux Act and the Fifteenth Amendment, protected local blacks in McIntosh County through his office as
justice of the peace, and involved himself in a plethora of
meetings and movements to improve the social, economic,
and political freedom of his race. His efforts helped lift
blacks toward freedom. Negotiation from strength did work.

But white Georgians redeemed state politics in the December 1870 election, and Campbell foresaw the reversal of

black advances. He predicted that the Redeemer freshet would quickly erode the gains that had been made by the Radical legislature. Campbell turned to the last available option open to him—black power. Through the unified efforts of McIntosh's black majority and in his role as justice of the peace, he forced whites to treat blacks with fairness.

Campbell led the black community toward equality. He believed in the Republican party motto, "Free Soil, Free Labor, Free Men," and he did much in the Georgia senate and in his many trips to Washington to encourage progressive reform and to keep the Radical spirit alive. On the local level in McIntosh County, Campbell never stopped being the freedmen's agent. He supported black rights and acted as the mediator in confrontations between management and labor, merchant and consumer, criminal and victim, and others. Campbell acted as labor adviser, political boss, spiritual overlord, black militant, and black protector. Through these roles, he consistently upheld and pursued the rights of blacks to equal treatment and respect. In so doing, his efforts oppressed the white community.

Campbell knew that to turn the freedmen into free men, white power must be subdued. He had to teach whites that any harsh treatment of his people would be met with arrests, jailings, fines, and threats of insurrection. To keep whites in line, Campbell drilled his militia and called frequent meetings. His actions not only consolidated the inner strength of the black machine, they also informed whites of the authority and hegemony he had usurped from them. He did not hesitate to arrest either foreign nationals or local whites who mistreated blacks or refused to respect his court. Campbell delayed the return of Democratic rule because of his willingness to confront whites with black power.

At the local level, he forestalled Redeemer rule for five years before a statewide conspiracy involving state, district, and local whites finally deposed him. In 1876 whites successfully confronted and triumphed over Campbell, but only by concerted effort. Governor James Smith ultimately ensured the success of the conspiracy when he appointed Henry Tompkins judge. Tompkins's single-minded zeal to remove Campbell rallied McIntosh whites to risk black riots and threats to reimplement white rule.

Yet even when the whites finally removed him from the county by putting him in the chain gang, Campbell's well-organized, racially unified machine withstood the onslaught. It remained an active force in McIntosh County politics for forty years. And although it was not exactly full-fledged Radicalism, the black machine successfully returned a black legislator to the General Assembly in every election, except for the decade of the 1890s, until 1907. In three of the five contests in the 1890s, the white winner owed his victory to black voters opposing Campbell's old rival, Lectured Crawford.[1]

That whites, who controlled the election manager positions, did not fraudulently fix returns in favor of white candidates demonstrates another part of Campbell's legacy. While raising the conditions of blacks by demanding fairer wages and better treatment from whites and by instilling in black minds bourgeois notions of education, morality, family, thrift, political involvement, hard work, and self-reliance, Campbell had focused white resentment not on his machine but on himself. Thus, when whites removed him from the county, they believed that they had reestablished their authority and the county had been redeemed. They did not challenge the black majority directly by reversing the gains of all black officeholders. Instead, fusion politics became the rule. With Campbell gone, whites compromised with the black machine and race relations in McIntosh County became surprisingly moderate. As long as blacks did not move to keep whites from all county positions, whites allowed them to remain in the posts of coroner, justice of the peace, and constable. This, of course, was tokenism, but it nevertheless gave blacks alternatives unavailable in an exclusively white structure.[2]

In 1882 Campbell returned to McIntosh County to oppose Lectured Crawford's bid for the state legislature, to campaign for the election of a Republican governor, and to support Chester Arthur's programs. Less than ten days after Campbell arrived in Darien, Judge Tompkins issued a bench warrant and had him arrested on the old charge of false imprisonment of John Fisher. This was Tompkins's way of warning Campbell against any effort to stir up black militancy. Because Campbell's arrest was just a warning, Tompkins set a comparatively low bail, $500, and Campbell soon went free.[3]

In early August Campbell attended the state Republican convention in Atlanta. He wanted to help bind the Republicans together, stop the factionalism between moderates and radicals, and deter any attempts at fusion with Democrats. No doubt he hoped to whip up rank-and-file support for a Republican governor as the only hope for overturning planter control. The *Atlanta Constitution* reported that "Tunis Campbell, an old colored man [seventy years old], made a good speech closely listened to by the delegates" and that he prayed for Chester Arthur, education, and harmony within the Republican party. The next month Campbell worked in Savannah for the election of Republican candidates to the United States Congress. His efforts to elect Republicans to the governorship and to national office failed, but he would enjoy success in McIntosh County.[4]

Referring to Campbell's six-year absence, the *Timber Gazette* proudly proclaimed: "Do not fear [Campbell] . . . he is not boss now." But blacks knew that Campbell had always championed their rights, and they quickly moved to support him. A Doboy rally resolved to "authorize Rev. T. G. Campbell, Sr., to act in all cases for us in this campaign and to carry out and make such arrangement as in his judgment will build up the Republican party." One month later, the *Timber Gazette,* obviously awed by Campbell's support among the black citizenry, reversed its earlier judgment: "The colored people of this county have the greatest confidence in Tunis G. Campbell, and are willing to let him . . . do just as his sweet will dictates. He is still strong in the hearts of the colored people and if he were eligible they would not hesitate for one moment to give him any office within their gift. Wonderful magnetism, curious people."[5]

On August 26 the *Timber Gazette* commented resignedly that Campbell had the power personally to select the McIntosh legislator and sighed: "We hope he picks a decent colored man." Campbell picked Hercules Wilson, one of his longtime supporters, and in the November election, Wilson easily defeated Crawford. Almost simultaneously, Tompkins, perhaps satisfied with Campbell's demeanor, or facing the reality that the statute of limitations had long since expired in the Fisher case, nolle-prossed the charge of false imprisonment.[6]

On December 30, 1882, Campbell made his farewell speech to McIntosh blacks and left the state. The events of his life for the next nine years remain veiled in obscurity. He died in Boston on December 4, 1891. His successes in Georgia provide a unique demonstration of the power one strong-willed black man could impose on a community torn by the new status of chattels-now-freedmen.[7]

In 1907, many years after Campbell left Georgia, the General Assembly disfranchised blacks and thereby destroyed the remnants of the McIntosh black machine. Over the years, memories of Campbell faded and a myth arose of a black carpetbagger who exploited black labor and confidence for his own benefit. That view is manifestly incorrect.[8] Campbell is important because his vision and efforts gave the just-freed blacks time to cope with the realities and terms of freedom and his actions gave them confidence to resist oppression. Instead of exploiting labor and confidence to selfish ends, he kept whites from taking advantage of blacks by exhorting the freedmen to be vigilant in their dealings with their old masters and with white opportunists from the North. Blacks confided in him because he acted in their behalf; they knew his speeches contained more than mere rhetoric. Campbell held black confidence because his actions had earned it.

NOTES

INTRODUCTION

1. As an introduction to these issues, see Emory M. Thomas, *The American War and Peace, 1860–1877* (Englewood Cliffs, N.J.: Prentice-Hall, 1973), pp. 173–210; and Numan V. Bartley, *The Creation of Modern Georgia* (Athens: University of Georgia Press, 1983), pp. 16–80.

2. Alan Conway, *The Reconstruction of Georgia* (Minneapolis: University of Minnesota Press, 1966), p. 22; Bessie Lewis, *They Called Their Town Darien: Being a Short History of Darien and McIntosh County, Georgia* (Darien, Ga.: Darien News, 1975), p. 55.

3. For an excellent description of the mechanics involved in rice growing, see Frances Butler Leigh, *Ten Years on a Georgia Plantation since the War* (1883; rpt. New York: Negro Universities Press, 1969), pp. 265–68; U.S. Department of Agriculture, *Report of the Commissioner of Agriculture for the Year 1867* (Washington, D.C.: U.S. Government Printing Office, 1867), 2:174–79.

4. George G. Smith, *The Story of Georgia and the Georgia People, 1732 to 1860* (Atlanta: Franklin Printing and Publishing Co., 1900), p. 214; Frances Anne Kemble, *Journal of a Residence on a Georgian Plantation in 1838–1839,* ed. John A. Scott (1863; rpt. Athens: University of Georgia Press, 1984), pp. 96–97; Ralph B. Flanders, *Plantation Slavery in Georgia* (Chapel Hill: University of North Carolina Press, 1933), pp. 229–30.

5. Phinizy Spalding, "Colonial Period," in Kenneth Coleman, ed., *A History of Georgia* (Athens: University of Georgia Press, 1977), pp. 35–37; petition quoted in Spencer B. King, *Darien: The Death and Rebirth of a Southern Town* (Macon, Ga.: Mercer University Press, 1981), pp. 6–7.

6. *Savannah Morning News,* September 6, 1872, p. 3, col. 1 (page and column hereafter indicated in parenthesis); 1860 Census, Population and Slave Schedules, Liberty County, Georgia; Burnette Vanstory, *Georgia's Land of the Golden Isles* (Athens: University of Georgia Press, 1981), pp. 57–60.

7. Kemble, *Journal,* p. xxxviii; 1850 Census, Slave Schedules, McIntosh County, Georgia; Vanstory, *Georgia's Land of the Golden Isles,* pp. 94–95, 104–6; Margaret Davis Cate, *Early Days of Coastal Georgia* (St. Simons Island, Ga.: Fort Frederica Association, 1955), pp. 59–61, 123.

8. Eric Foner, *Nothing But Freedom: Emancipation and Its Legacy* (Baton Rouge: Louisiana State University Press, 1983), p. 79; Charles Spalding Wylly, *Memories and Annals* (Brunswick, Ga.: Glover Bros., 1916), pp. 71–72; Flanders, *Plantation Slavery,* p. 82; 1860 Census, Population and Slave Schedules, McIntosh and Liberty counties, Georgia; *Annual Report of the Comptroller General of the State of Georgia, 1860* (Milledgeville, Ga.: Broughton, Nisbet, and Barnes, 1860), p. 42, lists 4,024 slaves in McIntosh County, valued at $2,152,250; *Georgia Official and Statistical Register, 1975–1976* (Atlanta: Perry Communications, 1976), pp. 1315, 1554.

9. George B. Bowen, "Survey of County and Municipal Fiscal Affairs: Narrative Report on McIntosh County, Georgia," WPA Report, undated, pp. 8–9.

10. George White, *Statistics of the State of Georgia* (Savannah: W. Thorne Williams, 1849), pp. 414–16; Bartley, *Creation,* p. 18; Georgia Bryan Conrad, *Reminiscences of a Southern Woman* (Hampton, Va.: Hampton Institute Press, 1901), p. 1; Vanstory, *Georgia's Land of the Golden Isles,* p. 81.

11. For an excellent discussion of carpetbaggers, see L. N. Powell, *New Masters: Northern Planters during the Civil War and Reconstruction* (New Haven: Yale University Press, 1980).

12. August Meier, "Afterward: New Perspectives on the Nature of Black Political Leadership during Reconstruction," in Howard N. Rabinowitz, ed., *Southern Black Leaders of the Reconstruction Era* (Urbana: University of Illinois Press, 1982), pp. 394–95.

13. Loren Schweninger, "James T. Rapier of Alabama and the Noble Cause of Reconstruction," in Rabinowitz, ed., *Southern*

Black Leaders, pp. 82, 95; William C. Harris, "Blanche K. Bruce of Mississippi: Conservative Assimilationist," in ibid., pp. 3, 6, 7, 12, 26–32; Thomas, *American War and Peace,* p. 197.

14. Peter S. Klingman, "Race and Faction in the Public Career of Florida's Josiah T. Walls," in Rabinowitz, ed., *Southern Black Leaders,* pp. 59–75; Oken Edet Uya, *From Slavery to Public Service: Robert Smalls, 1839–1915* (New York: Oxford University Press, 1971), pp. 11–31, 56–130.

15. *Darien Timber Gazette,* January 28 (3:3), February 4 (3:1), July 21 (3:1), August 11 (3:3), 1876; Tunis G. Campbell, *Sufferings of the Rev. T. G. Campbell and His Family in Georgia* (Washington, D.C.: Enterprise, 1877), pp. 25–26.

CHAPTER ONE

1. Tunis G. Campbell, *Sufferings of the Rev. T. G. Campbell and His Family in Georgia* (Washington, D.C.: Enterprise, 1877), p. 5.

2. Ibid.; *Report of the Joint Select Committee to Inquire into the Condition of Affairs in the Late Insurrectionary States,* 13 vols. (Washington, D.C.: U.S. Government Printing Office, 1872), 7:854 (hereafter cited as *Ku Klux Conspiracy*).

3. Campbell, *Sufferings,* pp. 5–6; *Ku Klux Conspiracy,* 7:854.

4. *Rochester North Star,* May 4, 1849 (2:2, 3:2).

5. *Frederick Douglass' Paper,* July 15, 1853 (3:2–5), 22, 1853 (1:2).

6. Ibid.; May 4, 1855 (3:7); *Rochester North Star,* May 4, 1849 (2:2, 3:2).

7. Campbell, *Sufferings,* p. 114; *Ku Klux Conspiracy,* 7:854; Tunis G. Campbell, *Hotel Keepers, Head Waiters, and Housekeepers' Guide* (Boston: Coolidge and Wiley, 1848); rpt. as *Never Let People Be Kept Waiting: A Textbook on Hotel Management,* ed. Doris Elizabeth King (Raleigh, N.C.: Graphic Press, 1973), pp. xxiii, 5, 114, 116–17.

8. Campbell, *Sufferings,* p. 7; *Ku Klux Conspiracy,* 7:854. I have been unable further to illuminate Campbell's personal life.

9. *Ku Klux Conspiracy,* 7:854.

10. *War of the Rebellion: A Compilation of the Official Records of the Union and Confederate Armies,* 128 vol. (Washington, D.C.: U.S. Government Printing Office, 1880–1901), 3d ser., 2:27–28, 152–53, 663–64 (hereafter cited as *OR*).

11. For an excellent study of contrabands in Georgia, see Clarence M. Mohr, "Georgia Blacks during Secession and Civil War, 1859–1865" (Ph.D. dissertation, University of Georgia, 1975); for insights into Saxton's role and the benefits the new freedmen gained at Port Royal, see Willie Lee Rose, *Rehearsal for Reconstruction: The Port Royal Experiment* (Indianapolis: Bobbs-Merrill, 1964), and Edwin D. Hoffman, "From Slavery to Self-Reliance: The Record of Achievement of the Freedmen of the Sea Island Region," *Journal of Negro History* 41 (January 1956):8–42; for an investigation into a similar experiment at Davis Bend, Mississippi, see Janet S. Hermann, *The Pursuit of a Dream* (New York: Oxford University Press, 1981).

12. *Rochester North Star,* May 4, 1849 (2:2, 3:2).

13. Rose, *Rehearsal,* pp. 43–44; James M. McPherson, "The Ballot and Land for the Freedmen, 1861–1865," in Kenneth M. Stampp and Leon F. Litwack, eds., *Reconstruction: An Anthology of Revisionist Writings* (Baton Rouge: Louisiana State University Press, 1969), pp. 145–46.

14. Rose, *Rehearsal,* pp. 240–41.

15. C. Vann Woodward, Introduction to ibid., p. xviii.

16. For Sherman's account of his march to Savannah and the official account, see William T. Sherman, *Memoirs of Gen. W. T. Sherman,* 2 vols. (New York: Charles L. Webster, 1891), 2:171–252; *OR,* 1st ser., 44:pt. 2, pp. 1–418.

17. W. T. Sherman to H. W. Halleck, January 12, 1865, *OR,* 1st ser., 47:pt. 2, p. 36; H. W. Halleck to W. T. Sherman, December 30, 1864, ibid., 44:836–37. Halleck asks, "Could not escaped slaves find, at least, a partial supply of food in the rice fields about Savannah, and occupation in the rice and cotton plantations on the coast?" Precedents for confiscation of rebel lands were the Confiscation Acts of August 6, 1861, and July 17, 1862. As early as December 14, 1863, a bill was introduced in the U.S. Congress to create a supervisory agency to manage the freed blacks and to al-

low them to occupy abandoned and confiscated lands. See George R. Bentley, *A History of the Freedmen's Bureau* (Philadelphia: University of Pennsylvania Press, 1955), p. 36.

18. *OR,* 1st ser., 47:pt. 2, pp. 37–41; Sherman, *Memoirs,* 2:245–47. James Lynch, a northern missionary, disagreed with Frazier about colonization; Lynch preferred to live among whites.

19. *OR,* 1st ser., 47:pt. 2, pp. 60–62; *Savannah Daily Herald,* January 24–31, 1865 (3:1, 2, or 3). For a succinct discussion of the Sherman reservation, see Claude F. Oubre, *Forty Acres and a Mule: The Freedmen's Bureau and Black Land Ownership* (Baton Rouge: Louisiana State University Press, 1978), pp. 18–19, 46–71.

20. Bentley, *History of the Freedmen's Bureau,* p. 49; James M. McPherson, *Ordeal by Fire: The Civil War and Reconstruction* (New York: Alfred A. Knopf, 1982), p. 401. McPherson notes that the bureau was proposed in 1863 but disagreement between House and Senate delayed its formation. See also "First Freedmen's Bureau Act," in Walter L. Fleming, ed., *Documentary History of Reconstruction: Political, Military, Social, Religious, Educational, and Industrial, 1865 to 1906* (New York: McGraw-Hill, 1966), pp. 319–20; General Order No. 91, May 12, 1865, *OR,* 1st ser., 47:pt. 3, p. 477.

21. Campbell, *Sufferings,* p. 7; *Ku Klux Conspiracy,* 7:846, 854. In October 1871, Campbell testified that he came to Georgia in 1864 (ibid., p. 846), but the correct date is 1865, as given in *Sufferings;* see "Roster of Civilians doing duty under control of Bvt. Maj. Gen. Rufus Saxton, Assistant Commissioner, August, 1865," Bureau of Refugees, Freedmen, and Abandoned Lands (hereafter BRFAL), Records of the Assistant Commissioner for the State of South Carolina, Record Group 105, National Archives, Washington, D.C., Microcopy 869, Roll 43, p. 6.

22. T. G. Campbell to New York Freedmen's Relief Association, April 13, 19, 1865, in Dorothy Sterling, ed., *The Trouble They Seen: Black People Tell the Story of Reconstruction* (Garden City, N.Y.: Doubleday, 1976), pp. 34–36.

23. Mohr, "Georgia Blacks," pp. 108–9.

24. Leon F. Litwack, *Been in the Storm So Long: The Aftermath of Slavery* (New York: Alfred A. Knopf, 1979), p. xiv; C. Vann Woodward, *Origins of the New South, 1877–1913* (Baton Rouge: Louisiana State University Press, 1951), p. 29.

25. Rufus Saxton, *General Orders, etc., Issued by Maj.-Gen. Rufus Saxton, as Military Governor, Department of the South and as Asst. Commissioner BRFAL of South Carolina, Georgia, and Florida, 1862–1866* (Washington, D.C.: n.p., 1867), p. 3; McPherson, "Ballot," pp. 153–54.

26. *Savannah Daily Herald,* April 23, 1865 (2:4).

27. Campbell, *Hotel Keepers,* p. 5; Tunis Campbell to A. P. Ketchum, June 30, 1865, Uncatalogued MSS Collection 2031, Freedmen's Bureau Records, Folder "St. Catherine's Island," Georgia Historical Society (hereafter GHS), Savannah, Ga.: Rufus Saxton to O. O. Howard, December 6, 1865, U.S. Congress, *Senate Executive Documents,* 39th Cong., 1st sess., pt. 2, p. 141.

28. *New York Herald,* June 13, 1866 (5:2); *Ku Klux Conspiracy,* 7:854, 937; E. Merton Coulter, "Tunis G. Campbell, Negro Reconstructionist in Georgia," *Georgia Historical Quarterly* 51 (December 1957): pp. 403–4; C. Mildred Thompson, *Reconstruction in Georgia: Economic, Social, Political, 1865–1872* (1915; rpt. Savannah: Beehive Press, 1972), p. 48; Betsy Fancher, *The Lost Legacy of Georgia's Golden Isles* (Garden City, N.Y.: Doubleday, 1971), p. 129; Campbell to Ketchum, June 30, 1865.

29. T. G. Campbell to asst. commissioner, June 16, 1865, BRFAL, Records of South Carolina, Roll 7, p. 225; Tunis Campbell to A. P. Ketchum, June 15, 1865, "St. Catherine's," GHS. In his letter of June 16, 1865, Campbell states that there were 309 freedmen on St. Catherines—8 fewer than he mentioned in his June 15 letter.

30. Campbell to Ketchum, June 15, 1865.

31. Coulter, "Campbell," p. 404; *Ku Klux Conspiracy,* 7:937.

32. Sherman's Order No. 15 established a reservation exclusively for freedmen; Saxton designed the supplement to keep white adventurers from entering the islands. See Oubre, *Forty Acres and a Mule,* pp. 49–67, for the best analysis of the debates over restoring land to former owners versus keeping promises to the freedmen. Oubre's discussion of the attempts of O. O. Howard and Rufus Saxton to circumvent presidential demands for restoration is insightful. He critically but sympathetically presents General Davis Tillson, assistant commissioner for Georgia, as a man trying to do his best for freedmen and planters but mistaken as to the fairness the workers would receive.

33. Campbell to Ketchum, June 2, 1865, "St. Catherine's," GHS; Campbell to Saxton, September 10, 1865, BRFAL, Records of South Carolina, Roll 7, p. 302.

34. Robert Higgs, *Competition and Coercion: Blacks in the American Economy, 1865–1914* (Cambridge: Cambridge University Press, 1977), pp. 118–22.

35. Campbell to Ketchum, June 20, 30, 1865; Campbell to Saxton, September 10, 1865; Tunis Campbell to American Missionary Association, April 11, 1866, "Letters from Georgia," American Missionary Association Archives, Microfilm, No. 23320 (hereafter AMA), Amistad Research Center, Dillard University, New Orleans; "School Reports: Georgia, November 1865–December 1870," BRFAL, Records of the Education Division of the Bureau of Refugees, Freedmen, and Abandoned Lands, 1865–1871, Microcopy 803, Roll 19, pp. 282, 288, 291; Albert Colbey Smith, "Down Freedom's Road: The Contours of Race, Class, and Property Crime in Black-Belt Georgia, 1860–1915" (Ph.D. dissertation, University of Georgia, 1982), p. 123; Sterling, ed., *Trouble,* p. 15.

36. Eric Foner, *Nothing But Freedom: Emancipation and Its Legacy* (Baton Rouge: Louisiana State University Press, 1983), pp. 13, 20, 40; Foner's thesis fitting freedmen into the classic republican synthesis is deftly explained in his first chapter, pp. 8–38.

37. Campbell, Monthly Report, December 15, 1865, BRFAL, Records of South Carolina, Roll 33, pp. 95–96; Eaton, Monthly Report, October 15, 1865, ibid., pp. 57–58; Oubre, *Forty Acres and a Mule,* p. 64.

38. Robert P. Brooks, *The Agrarian Revolution in Georgia, 1865–1912* (Madison: University of Wisconsin Press, 1914), p. 109; W. Swinton McIntosh, "McIntosh County and Her Resources," in McIntosh County, City Court Records, Georgia Department of Archives and History, Atlanta (hereafter GDAH); Thompson, *Reconstruction in Georgia,* p. 357; Edward J. Thomas, *Memoirs of a Southerner, 1840–1923* (Savannah: By the author, 1923), p. 10.

39. Thomas P. Janes, *A Manual of Georgia for the Use of Immigrants and Capitalists* (Atlanta: Harrison, 1878), p. 85.

40. Campbell to Saxton, September 10, 1865.

41. Campbell, Monthly Report, December 15, 1865, BRFAL, Records of South Carolina, Roll 33, pp. 95–96; *New York Herald,* June 13, 1866 (5:2); Oubre, *Forty Acres and a Mule,* p. 63; Thompson,

Reconstruction in Georgia, p. 48; Coulter, "Campbell," p. 405; James L. Roark, *Masters without Slaves: Southern Planters in the Civil War and Reconstruction* (New York: Norton, 1977), p. 112.

42. W.E.B. DuBois, *Black Reconstruction in America: An Essay toward a History of the Part Which Black Folk Played in the Attempt to Reconstruct Democracy in America, 1860–1880* (New York: Atheneum, 1979), identifies the central issue of Reconstruction as the struggle over land and labor. See also George A. Rogers and R. Frank Saunders, eds., *Swampwater and Wiregrass: Historical Sketches of Coastal Georgia* (Macon, Ga.: Mercer University Press, 1984), p. 157; Liberty County, Ga., Population and Slave Schedules, 1860 Census; *Savannah Daily Herald,* June 28, 1865 (4:2).

43. E. A. Wild to Rufus Saxton, July 14, 1865, BRFAL, Records of South Carolina, Roll 34, p. 177; A. P. Ketchum to Rufus Saxton, September 1, 1865, ibid., pp. 269–70.

44. Tunis Campbell to A. P. Ketchum, July 17, 1865, "St. Catherine's," GHS.

45. J. S. Fullerton to O. O. Howard, July 22, 23, 1865, BRFAL, Registers and Letters Received by the Commissioner, Micro. 752, Roll 14, pp. 1350, 1367, 1369, 1372.

46. Oubre, *Forty Acres and a Mule,* p. 49; "Reports of the Assistant Commissioners of the Freedmen's Bureau," U.S. Congress, *Senate Executive Documents,* 39th Cong., 1st sess., pt. 2, No. 27 (serial 1238), pp. 140–41; "Freedmen's Affairs," U.S. Congress, *Senate Executive Documents,* 39th Cong., 2d sess., No. 6 (serial 1276), pp. 52–54; Dwight B. Billings, Jr., *Planters and the Making of a "New South": Class, Politics, and Development in North Carolina, 1865–1900* (Chapel Hill: University of North Carolina Press, 1979), p. 101. For a discussion of Saxton's attempts to protect the freedmen's right to the land and Tillson's one-mindedness toward contracts, see Oubre, *Forty Acres and a Mule,* pp. 49–59, 62–67; Oliver Otis Howard, *Autobiography of Oliver Otis Howard, Major General United States Army,* 2 vols. (New York: Baker & Taylor, 1907), 2:286.

47. Litwack, *Been in the Storm So Long,* pp. 386, 408; Lewis N. Wynne, "Planter Politics in Georgia, 1860–1890" (Ph.D. dissertation, University of Georgia, 1980), p. 96.

48. In his *Autobiography,* Howard explained Johnson's attitude

toward Saxton: "The President was very anxious to be rid of every prominent officer who was reported to have been long the freedman's friend. In his eyes . . . Saxton . . . [was] too pronounced in behalf of those assailed . . . [he was] too much the advocate of . . . [his black] wards to suit the situation" (2:283–84). See also Edwin D. Hoffman, "From Slavery to Self-Reliance: The Record of Achievement of the Freedmen of the Sea Island Region," *Journal of Negro History* 41 (January 1956):8–42. William S. McFeely, *Yankee Stepfather: General O. O. Howard and the Freedmen* (New Haven: Yale University Press, 1968), pp. 119–29, summarizes the personalities and aims of Saxton, Tillson, and Fullerton. Tillson quoted from "Freedmen's Affairs," pp. 52–53; Oubre, *Forty Acres and a Mule,* pp. 63–64.

49. "Roster of Civilians Employed during the Month of January 1866," BRFAL, Records of South Carolina, Roll 43, p. 53; "Reports of the Assistant Commissioners," pp. 103, 106; Campbell, *Sufferings,* p. 8.

50. *New York Herald,* June 13, 1866 (5:2); Oubre, *Forty Acres and a Mule,* pp. 62, 64–65; "Reports of the Assistant Commissioners," pp. 104–5; "Freedmen's Affairs," p. 54. On the discussion of Campbell's authority to grant land, verbally given by Saxton, and Tillson's ultimate agreement to grant freedmen with "Campbell titles" ten to fifteen acres, see Oubre, *Forty Acres and a Mule,* pp. 49, 51, 59; Tillson to Howard, April 13, 1866, BRFAL, Records of the Commissioner, Micro. 752, Roll 27, pp. 559–63; Tillson to Howard, February 12, 1866, Roll 20, pp. 1074–78. Before November 1867, the Winchester and Schuyler enterprise on St. Catherines failed—Winchester died, and Schuyler, bankrupt returned North owing the freedmen at least $1,852.58. There is evidence to suggest two other partners, C. Prince and Mr. Ballard; both first names unknown (J. M. Hoag to C. C. Sibley, November 18, 1867, "St. Catherine's," GHS). I have been unable to locate Schuyler's first name.

51. "Reports of the Assistant Commissioners," p. 54; Oubre, *Forty Acres and a Mule,* p. 66.

52. *New York Herald,* June 13, 1866 (5:2). Winchester and Schuyler's 1867 contract stipulated that the workers would get "substantial rations" consisting of twelve quarts of corn, two

pounds of bacon per week, one-half gallon of syrup and one pint of salt per month to be deducted from a one-fourth share of the crop ("BelleVille," GHS); Jacqueline Jones, *Soldiers of Light and Love: Northern Teachers and Georgia Blacks, 1865–1873* (Chapel Hill: University of North Carolina Press, 1980), pp. 55, 59.

53. T. G. Campbell to Rufus Saxton, March 29, 1866, BRFAL, Records of the Commissioner, Micro. 752, Roll 27, pp. 559–63; Davis Tillson to O. O. Howard, April 13, 1866, ibid., Roll 4, p. 111; R. K. Scott to O. O. Howard, April 26, 1866, BRFAL, Records of South Carolina, Roll 3, p. 145; Campbell, *Sufferings,* p. 8; Special Order No. 130, September 5, 1866, BRFAL, Records of the Commissioner, Micro. 752, Roll 37, p. 1065.

54. Affidavit of Toby Maxwell, Tunis Campbell file, GDAH; BRFAL, Records of Education, Roll 19, pp. 291, 322; Coulter, "Campbell," p. 405; Smith, "Down Freedom's Road," p. 123.

55. William Cooke Plantation Book, 1861–67, p. 102, University of Georgia Library, Athens; *New York Herald,* June 13, 1866 (5:2); "Report of Abandoned and Confiscated Lands for the Month of August 1865," BRFAL, Records of South Carolina, Roll 33, pp. 1–2; "Reports of Conditions and Operations, July 1865–December 1866," ibid., Roll 34, p. 35. I have been unable to determine the first names of McBride and Dickson.

56. "Reports of the Assistant Commissioners," pp. 125–26. For land titles issued to the freedmen on Sapelo and St. Catherines and marked "Restored" to former owners, see "Register of Land Titles Issued to Freedmen," BRFAL, Records of Georgia, Micro. 798, Roll 36, pp. 22, 27. Many freedmen left the "reservation" after learning that the land was to be restored. The *Savannah Daily Herald,* November 11, 1865 (3:1), reports that on the previous day eighty freedmen left St. Simons, St. Catherines, and Ossabaw "after learning that the land would be surrendered to its original owners."

57. L. N. Powell, *New Masters: Northern Planters during the Civil War and Reconstruction* (New Haven: Yale University Press, 1980), pp. 87–93; Affidavit of Toby Maxwell, Tunis Campbell file.

58. Davis Tillson to O. O. Howard, September 22, 1866, BRFAL, Registers and Letters Received by the Commissioner, Micro. 752, Roll 5, p. 408, Roll 37, pp. 1061–64.

59. Ibid., Roll 37, pp. 1061–64; *New York Herald,* June 13, 1866 (5:2); Affidavit of Remus Elliot, Tunis Campbell file; McFeely, *Yankee Stepfather,* pp. 247–58.

60. Tillson to Howard, September 22, 1866, p. 1065.

61. Campbell, *Sufferings,* p. 8; T. G. Campbell to O. O. Howard, January 25, 1867, BRFAL, Records of the Commissioner, Micro. 752, Roll 6, p. 113; Affidavits of Toby Maxwell and John Roberts, Tunis Campbell file; Tunis Campbell to J. R. Lewis, December 1867, "BelleVille," GHS. In 1871, Campbell and Hopkins disputed whether the land had been bought or leased; Campbell insisted that it was a purchase agreement. He indicated that a unique "cropping-to-owning" (rent-to-buy) arrangement had been reached, in which he agreed to pay the rent of one-third share to Hopkins and "Payment of the first installment of $5000 dollars to Mr. Hopkins." Campbell certainly believed he was buying the land, but when Hopkins balked in 1871, the court decided in his favor. For a discussion of why southern planters rented or sold land to northerners, see Powell, *New Masters,* pp. 48–50.

62. Campbell, *Sufferings,* p. 8; Campbell to Lewis, December 1867; *Ku Klux Conspiracy,* 7:861.

63. Joel Williamson, *The Crucible of Race: Black-White Relations in the American South since Emancipation* (New York: Oxford University Press, 1984), pp. 44–49.

64. Campbell to Howard, January 25, 1867; J. M. Hoag to Charles R. Holcombe, July 11, 1867, "BelleVille," GHS.

65. Sterling, ed., *Trouble,* pp. 248–51.

66. Ibid.

67. Ibid., p. 251.

68. *Savannah Daily Republican,* August 18, 1867 (2:2).

69. Agreement between Tunis Campbell and BelleVille Colony, "BelleVille," GHS.

70. Tunis Campbell to J. M. Hoag, June 1, 1867, ibid.; J. M. Hoag to Charles R. Holcombe, July 11, 1867, ibid.; Affidavit of Toby Maxwell, Tunis Campbell file.

71. Giles Pease to S. S. Jocelyn, March 25, 1868, "Letters from Georgia," AMA Archives, Microfilm, No. 21375.

72. Campbell to Lewis, December 1867.

73. Ibid.

74. J. M. Hoag to C. C. Sibley, November 30, 1867.

75. Tunis Campbell to J. M. Hoag, November 4, 1867, "Belle-Ville," GHS. Campbell's letter of December 1867 to J. R. Lewis reported the harvest of 9,300 pounds of cotton and 505 bushels of shelled corn instead of the figures quoted by Hoag; in any case, it did not pay for the advanced rations.

76. Campbell to Lewis, December 1867; Affidavit of Toby Maxwell, Tunis Campbell file.

CHAPTER TWO

1. Walter L. Fleming, ed., *Documentary History of Reconstruction: Political, Military, Social, Religious, Educational, and Industrial, 1865 to 1906,* 2 vols. (New York: McGraw-Hill, 1966), 1:401–3, 407–11, 415–18.

2. Jack B. Scroggs, "Carpetbagger Influence in the Political Reconstruction of the South Atlantic States, 1865–1876" (Ph.D. dissertation, University of North Carolina, 1951), p. 54.

3. Fleming, ed., *Documentary History,* pp. 430–33; C. Mildred Thompson, *Reconstruction in Georgia: Economic, Social, Political, 1865–1872* (1915; rpt. Savannah: Beehive Press, 1972), p. 169; General Order No. 5, April 8, 1867, U.S. Congress, *Senate Executive Documents,* 40th Cong., 1st sess., No. 14 (serial 1308), pp. 109–10, 117–21; Tunis G. Campbell, *Sufferings of the Rev. T. G. Campbell and His Family in Georgia* (Washington, D.C.: Enterprise, 1877), p. 9; Georgia Reconstruction Registration Record, District 2, McIntosh County, Georgia Department of Archives and History, Atlanta (hereafter GDAH); Allen D. Candler, ed., *The Confederate Records of the State of Georgia,* 5 vols. (Atlanta: State Printer, 1910), 5:100–105; *Savannah Daily Republican,* June 1, 1867 (3:1).

4. Fleming, ed., *Documentary History,* 1:431–32; Reconstruction Registration Record, McIntosh County.

5. Scroggs, "Carpetbagger Influence," p. 91; Fleming, ed., *Documentary History,* 1:432.

6. Theodore Maxwell Lawe, "The Black Reconstructionist in Georgia: 1865–1877" (M.A. thesis, Atlanta University, 1966), pp. 9–10.

7. *Savannah Daily Republican,* April 18, 1867 (2:1).

8. Ibid., April 23, (2:2), May 7, 1867 (1:2).

9. *Augusta Weekly Loyal Georgian,* July 6, 1867 (1:1, 1:3, 1:4).

10. Ibid.,; August 10, 1867 (1:1).

11. *Savannah Daily Republican,* July 8, 1867 (1:3, 2:2).

12. Edmund L. Drago, *Black Politicians and Reconstruction in Georgia: A Splendid Failure* (Baton Rouge: Louisiana State University Press, 1982), p. 34; E. Merton Coulter, "Tunis G. Campbell, Negro Reconstructionist in Georgia," *Georgia Historical Quarterly* 51 (December 1967):407, lists 169 delegates instead of 170; *Report of the Joint Select Committee to Inquire into the Condition of Affairs in the Late Insurrectionary States,* 13 vols. (Washington, D.C.: U.S. Government Printing Office, 1872), 7:855 (hereafter *Ku Klux Conspiracy*). Campbell stated that two whites voted in McIntosh, but those two voted in Liberty County according to the *Report of Madison Bell, Comptroller General of the State of Georgia, Covering the Period from August 11, 1868, to January 1, 1869* (Atlanta: Samuel Bard, Public Printer, 1869), Table A.

13. Alton Hornsby, Jr., "Turner, Henry McNeal," and Richard L. Hume, "Bradley, Aaron Alpeoria," in Kenneth Coleman and Charles S. Gurr, eds., *Dictionary of Georgia Biography,* 2 vols. (Athens: University of Georgia Press, 1983), 1:109, 2:1008–9; Numan V. Bartley, *The Creation of Modern Georgia* (Athens: University of Georgia Press, 1983), pp. 52–55; see Joseph P. Reidy, "Aaron A. Bradley: Voice of Black Labor in the Georgia Lowcountry," in Howard N. Rabinowitz, ed., *Southern Black Leaders of the Reconstruction Era* (Urbana: University of Illinois Press, 1982), pp. 281–308, for a summary of Bradley's character and programs.

14. Drago, *Black Politicians,* pp. 39–47; Ethel M. Christler, "Participation of Negroes in the Government of Georgia, 1867–1870" (M.A. thesis, Atlanta University, 1932), p. 6; *Journal of the Proceedings of the Constitutional Convention of the People of Georgia Held in the City of Atlanta in the Months of December 1867, and January, February, and March, 1868* (Augusta, Ga.: E. H. Pughe, 1868), pp. 294–97; Thompson, *Reconstruction in Georgia,* p. 173.

15. *Savannah Daily Republican,* December 12 (1:2), December 13 (2:1), quoting the *Atlanta Intelligencer,* December 10, 1867; *Journal of the Convention,* pp. 9, 14, 615–16; Coulter, "Campbell," p. 408.

16. Paul L. Sanford, "The Negro in the Political Reconstruction of Georgia, 1865–1872" (M.A. thesis, Atlanta University, 1947), pp. 16–17; *Savannah Daily Herald,* December 19, 1867 (1:2); *Journal of the Convention,* pp. 36, 279; Susie K. Taylor, *Reminiscences of My Life in Camp with the 33rd United States Colored Troops, Late 1st S.C. Volunteers* (1902; rpt. New York: Arno Press, 1968), p. 53.

17. *Journal of the Convention,* pp. 41, 151, 158; *Savannah Daily Republic,* December 18 (1:1) and 20, 1867 (1:2).

18. *Journal of the Convention,* pp. 159, 176, 216–17.

19. Ibid., pp. 148, 299–300, 311–12; Alan Conway, *The Reconstruction of Georgia* (Minneapolis: University of Minnesota Press, 1966), pp. 154–55.

20. Charles E. Wynes, "The Politics of Reconstruction, Redemption, and Bourbonism," in Kenneth Coleman, ed., *A History of Georgia* (Athens: University of Georgia Press, 1977), p. 212; James L. Owens, "The Negro in Georgia during Reconstruction, 1864–1872: A Social History" (Ph.D. dissertation, University of Georgia, 1975), p. 195.

21. *Journal of the Senate of the State of Georgia, 1868* (Macon, Ga.: J. W. Burke, 1868), pp. 11–12, 81.

22. Ibid., pp. 103, 162, 170, 265, 270, 414; Coulter, "Campbell," p. 409. For the problems blacks had in securing adequate passage between Savannah and Darien, see Taylor, *Reminiscences of My Life in Camp,* p. 63; John M. Matthews, "The Negro in Georgia Politics, 1865–1880" (M.A. thesis, Duke University, 1967), pp. 70–71; Margaret Mitchell, *Gone With the Wind* (1936; rpt. New York: Macmillan, 1964), p. 904.

23. *Journal of the Senate of Georgia, 1868,* pp. 84–86.

24. *Atlanta Constitution,* July 10, 1868 (1:4).

25. Thompson, *Reconstruction in Georgia,* pp. 193–96; Sanford, "Negro in Political Reconstruction," p. 33; Coulter, "Campbell," pp. 409–13; Conway, *Reconstruction of Georgia,* pp. 165–66; *Journal of the Senate of Georgia, 1868,* pp. 122–27, 138. In his autobiography, Campbell mistakenly says that he contended for the right of black officeholding for nine days in succession; he meant nine days in total (*Sufferings,* p. 9).

26. *Journal of the Senate of Georgia, 1868,* pp. 243–44, 273, 278–79; *Comptroller General's Report, 1869,* Table A.

27. Campbell, *Sufferings,* pp. 9–10; *Ku Klux Conspiracy,* 7:847;

Coulter, "Campbell," p. 414; quotes from Edward McPherson, ed., *The Political History of the United States of America during the Period of Reconstruction* (Washington, D.C.: Solomons & Chapman, 1875), p. 399; and *Journal of the Convention*, p. 158.

28. *Ku Klux Conspiracy*, 7:847, 854–56, 942.

29. Spencer Bidwell King, *Darien: The Death and Rebirth of a Southern Town* (Macon, Ga.: Mercer University Press, 1981), pp. 3, 64–73; *The Statistics of Population of the United States, 9th Census* (Washington, D.C.: U.S. Government Printing Office, 1872), p. 104.

30. Slave Schedules, McIntosh County, Georgia, 1860, Microfilm, U.S. Department of Commerce, Bureau of the Census; interview with Jim Cook, Ardock, Georgia, May 16, 1984. Cook's parents were Gignilliat slaves before and during the Civil War. He said they got their one hundred acres in exchange for one hundred bushels of sweet potatoes but lost the land when the taxes went unpaid. See also Last Will of Margaret Ann Harris, in Bessie Lewis Papers, Georgia Historical Society, Savannah; Wills of S. W. Wilson and Georgia Atkinson, Darien, Ga., Court of the Ordinary, "Record of Wills: May, 1873–November, 1915," pp. 12, 22.

31. Minnie C. Owen to E. P. Smith, March 7, 1870, "Letters from Georgia," American Missionary Association Archives, Microfilm, No. 23320, Amistad Research Center, Dillard University, New Orleans; Myrtie L. Candler, "Reminiscences of Life in Georgia, 1864–9," *Georgia Historical Quarterly* 34 (March 1950):13.

32. Manuel Gottlieb, "The Land Question in Georgia during Reconstruction," *Science and Society* 3 (Summer 1939):356; Horace M. Bond, "Social and Economic Forces in Alabama Reconstruction," in Kenneth M. Stampp and Leon F. Litwack, eds., *Reconstruction: An Anthology of Revisionist Writings* (Baton Rouge: Louisiana State University Press, 1969), pp. 373–74; Edward J. Thomas, *Memoirs of a Southerner, 1840–1923* (Savannah: By the author, 1923), pp. 40, 57; Albert Colbey Smith, "Down Freedom's Road: The Contours of Race, Class, and Property Crime in Black-Belt Georgia, 1860–1915" (Ph.D. dissertation, University of Georgia, 1982), p. 121.

33. Stephen J. DeCanio, *Agriculture in the Postbellum South: The Economics of Production and Supply* (Cambridge, Mass.: MIT Press, 1974), p. 220; Frances Butler Leigh, *Ten Years on a Georgia Plantation since the War* (1883; rpt. New York: Negro Universities

Press, Greenwood Publishing Corp., 1969), pp. 14, 21, 55–56; interview with Jim Cook, May 16, 1984.

34. Leigh, *Ten Years on a Georgia Planation,* p. 79; Thomas F. Armstrong, "From Task Labor to Free Labor: The Transition along Georgia's Rice Coast, 1820–1880," *Georgia Historical Quarterly* 54 (Winter 1980):440–43; Arnold H. Taylor, *Travail and Triumph: Black Life and Culture in the South since the Civil War* (Westport, Conn.: Greenwood Press, 1976), p. 69; Enoch M. Banks, *The Economics of Land Tenure in Georgia* (New York: Columbia University Press, 1905), p. 68; Charles L. Flynn, Jr., *White Land, Black Labor: Caste and Class in Late Nineteenth-Century Georgia* (Baton Rouge: Louisiana State University Press, 1983), pp. 4, 64–65; Charlton W. Tebeau, "The Planter in the Lower South, 1865–1880" (Ph.D. dissertation, University of Iowa, 1933), p. 112.

35. L. J. Alston and Robert Higgs, "Contractual Mix in Southern Agriculture since the Civil War: Facts, Hypotheses, and Tests," *Journal of Economic History* 42 (June 1982):334; Taylor, *Travail and Triumph,* p. 75; Willard Range, *A Century of Georgia Agriculture, 1850–1950* (Athens: University of Georgia Press, 1954), pp. 71, 84. For a good discussion of sharecropping see Lewis N. Wynne, "The Role of the Freedmen in the Post-Bellum Cotton Economy of Georgia," *Phylon* 42 (December 1981):312–15; Eric Foner, "Reconstruction Revisited," *Reviews in American History* 10 (December 1982):93.

36. Samuel A. Drake, *Georgia: Its History, Condition, and Resources* (New York: Charles Scribners' Sons, 1879), p. 12; Owens, "Negro in Georgia," pp. 81–82; Steven W. Engerrand, " 'Now Scratch or Die': The Genesis of Capitalistic Agricultural Labor in Georgia, 1865–1880" (Ph.D. dissertation, University of Georgia, 1981), p. 14; Armstrong, "From Task Labor to Free Labor," p. 440; Tebeau, "Planter in the Lower South," p. 107; Alston and Higgs, "Contractual Mix," p. 336.

37. Robert Higgs, *Competition and Coercion: Blacks in the American Economy, 1865–1914* (Cambridge: Cambridge University Press, 1977), pp. 37–61; Booker T. Washington and W.E.B. Du-Bois, *The Negro in the South: His Economic Progress in Relation to His Moral and Religious Development* (Philadelphia: George W. Jacobs, 1906), p. 46. From the planters' point of view, staple crop agriculture required a stable labor force which the fluidity of a

free, noncontract market would not sustain. The lack of capital prevented hiring hundreds of rice workers on a wage labor system, so contracts had to be compelling if the enterprise were to succeed. Unfortunately for the honest white landlords, too many planters cheated the freedmen in their contracts for Campbell to see anything but evil in the system. See Oscar Zeichner, "The Transition from Slave to Free Agricultural Labor in the Southern States," *Agricultural History* 13 (January 1939):22–32.

38. Affidavits of Samuel Ross, Allen Gould, James Steel, Nero West, Samuel Patterson, Lectured Crawford, and Remus Elliot, Tunis Campbell file, Georgia Department of Archives and History, Atlanta (hereafter GDAH).

39. William R. Gignilliat to R. E. Lester, January 1871, Tunis Campbell file; Leigh, *Ten Years on a Georgia Plantation,* p. 135.

40. Leigh, *Ten Years on a Georgia Plantation,* pp. 121, 128, 146–47, 168, 202–6. Barnwell later solved his labor problems by leasing convicts (sixty-four in 1876) from the state penitentiary (Department of Corrections, Account Book of Convicts Leased, 1872–1876, GDAH).

41. Tunis G. Campbell, *Hotel Keepers, Head Waiters, and Housekeepers' Guide* (Boston: Coolidge and Wiley, 1848); rpt. as *Never Let People Be Kept Waiting: A Textbook on Hotel Management,* ed. Doris Elizabeth King (Raleigh, N.C.: Graphic Press, 1973), pp. 6–7.

42. Campbell, *Sufferings,* p. 3.

43. Ibid.

44. Bureau of Refugees, Freedmen, and Abandoned Lands (hereafter BRFAL), Records of the Surgeon-in-Chief for the State of Georgia, 1865–1868, Record Group 105, National Archives, Washington, D.C., 9 rolls; "Roster of Officers and Civilian Agents, Dec. 1, 1867," George Wagner Papers, University of Georgia, Athens; "Roster of Officers and Civilian Agents, Sept. 1, 1868," BRFAL, Records of the Assistant Commissioner for the State of South Carolina, Micro. 869, Roll 35; BRFAL, *Records of the Education Division, 1865–1871,* Micro. 803, Roll 19, pp. 335, 348, 607, 615.

45. "Letters from Georgia," AMA Archives, Microfilm, Nos. 21177, 21333, 21803, 22220, 22241, 22402, 22939, 23139.

46. Susan P. Harrold to E. P. Smith, April 12, 1869, ibid., No. 22354.

47. In 1868, the two black teachers in Darien, Mrs. Thorpe and Miss Labbattie, taught approximately twenty-four students (Giles Pease to George Whipple, March 4, 1868, ibid., No. 21333). In January 1869, Mrs. Thorpe and Miss Labbattie were teaching three hundred students (J. M. Hoag to J. R. Lewis, January 19, 1869, Uncatalogued MSS collection 2031, Freedmen's Bureau, "McIntosh County," Georgia Historical Society, Savannah; Reconstruction Registration Oath Books, 1867–68, District 2, McIntosh County, GDAH).

48. *Statistics of Population, 1870,* 1:21–22, 625; Reconstruction Registration Record Book, McIntosh County.

49. Smith, "Down Freedom's Road," p. 120; Alexander St. Clair Abrams, *Manual and Biographical Register of the State of Georgia, 1871–2* (Atlanta: Plantation Press, 1872), p. 114.

50. Smith, "Down Freedom's Road," p. 124.

51. Ibid., p. 142.

52. Population Schedule, 1870, McIntosh County, U.S. Bureau of the Census. A good description of taking timber downstream to Darien and life there, in novel form, is Brainard Cheney, *River Rogue* (1942; rpt. Washington, D.C.: Burr Oak Publishers, 1982). A good historical account is Carlton A. Morrison, "Raftsmen of the Altamaha" (M.A. thesis, University of Georgia, 1970). By 1878, Darien had seven steam sawmills employing 125 hands and was the largest lumber port on the South Atlantic coast. See Thomas P. Janes, *A Manual of Georgia for Use of Immigrants and Capitalists* (Atlanta: Jas. P. Harrison, 1878), p. 88.

53. Affidavits of Samuel Ross and Toby Maxwell, Tunis Campbell file; *Ku Klux Conspiracy,* 7:861–62.

54. Smith, "Down Freedom's Road," p. 124; Drago, *Black Politicians,* pp. 51, 162.

55. James S. Allen, *Reconstruction: The Battle for Democracy, 1865–1876* (New York: International Publishers, 1937), p. 8; Affidavit of Hamilton Jackson, Tunis Campbell file.

56. Lt. J. H. Bradley to Col. J. H. Taylor, June 13, 1870, Tunis Campbell file; Allen, *Reconstruction,* p. 8.

57. Department of Corrections, Inmate Administration Division, Central Register of Convicts, 1866–79, vol. 3, line 30, GDAH; *Augusta Weekly Constitutionalist,* January 19, 1870 (4:2); *Savan-*

nah Morning News, June 28, 1872 (3:2), May 15, 1875 (3:2). Physical descriptions of Campbell are limited to one 1848(?) drawing used as frontispiece in his *Hotel Keepers* book, the one recorded by the Central Register of Convicts at his induction in 1876, and many, mostly vituperative, representations in Democratic newspapers. See Thomas Holt, *Black over White: Negro Political Leadership in South Carolina during Reconstruction* (Urbana: University of Illinois Press, 1977), pp. 61–62, for a discussion of how shades of color—black, brown, mulatto—influenced the freedmen's feelings about other blacks. Holt found that a "black" had more influence among the coastal Negroes than a "brown" or a "mulatto." Campbell's blackness probably boosted his success among coastal Georgians of Gullah ancestry.

58. U.S. Congress, *House Miscellaneous Documents,* 40th Cong., 3d sess., no. 52 (serial 1385), p. 91; Campbell, *Sufferings,* p. 10.

59. Campbell, *Sufferings,* pp. 10–12; *Atlanta Daily New Era,* January 11, 1870 (2:2); *Journal of the Senate of the State of Georgia, 1870,* pt. 1, pp. 24–25, 29; I. W. Avery, *The History of the State of Georgia from 1850 to 1881, Embracing the Three Important Epochs: The Decade before the War of 1861–5; The War; The Period of Reconstruction* (New York: Brown & Derby, 1881), p. 428; U.S. Congress, *Senate Executive Documents,* 41st Cong., 2d sess., no. 41 (serial 1406), pp. 11–12; *Atlanta Daily New Era,* January 30, 1870 (2:4).

60. *Journal of the Senate of Georgia, 1870,* 1:42, 362.

61. Ibid., pp. 102, 375; 2:9, 216.

62. Ibid., 1:368; 2:26–27, 215–16, 262, 297; 3:54, 291; *Acts and Resolutions of the General Assembly of the State of Georgia, 1870* (Atlanta: Public Printer, 1870), p. 186.

63. *Journal of the Senate of Georgia, 1870,* 2:215–16; 3:14, 32, 37–39, 262; *Savannah Morning News,* August 25, 1870 (2:2–3).

64. *Washington New Era,* March 17, 1870 (3:1, 3:4); *Atlanta Daily New Era,* March 12 (2:5), 17 (2:5), 19 (2:5), 30, 1870 (4:4); Campbell, *Sufferings,* p. 13.

65. *Atlanta Daily New Era,* February 2 (3:2), 3 (3:2), 4, 1871 (3:3); *Atlanta Constitution,* February 3, 1871 (3:1–2).

66. *Atlanta Daily New Era,* February 4, 1871 (3:3).

67. Ibid.

68. Ibid.; Campbell, *Sufferings,* p. 13; Coulter, "Campbell," p. 419; *Ku Klux Conspiracy,* 7:847.

69. *Atlanta Constitution,* February 3, 1871 (3:2).

CHAPTER THREE

1. Robert Penn Warren, Introduction to Brainard Cheney, *River Rogue* (1942; rpt. Washington, D.C.: Burr Oak Publishers, 1982), p. vii.

2. J. W. Leigh, *Other Days* (New York: Macmillan, 1921), p. 147; *Savannah Morning News,* August 18, 1871 (3:1); *Report of the Joint Select Committee to Inquire into the Condition of Affairs in the Late Insurrectionary States* (hereafter *Ku Klux Conspiracy*), 13 vols. (Washington, D.C.: U.S. Government Printing Office, 1872), 7:850, 856–57, 1058; E. Merton Coulter, "Tunis G. Campbell, Negro Reconstructionist in Georgia," *Georgia Historical Quarterly* 52 (March 1968):20.

3. Arrest warrant for John Irvine, July 14, 1871, Affidavit of Alonzo Guyton, Bill of Costs, all in Tunis Campbell file, Georgia Department of Archives and History, Atlanta (hereafter GDAH); *Atlanta Daily New Era,* August 11, 1871 (1:3). Under Georgia law, a justice of the peace was not allowed to set charges above $100 in any one case, but because five cases were involved, the charge can be misleading. Coulter considered Campbell's total bill of $193.28 "wholly illegal" ("Campbell," p. 21); *Ku Klux Conspiracy,* 7:857, 863.

4. Affidavit of John Irvine, Tunis Campbell file; *Savannah Morning News,* August 15, 1871 (3:1); *Atlanta Daily New Era,* August 17 (1:2), 18 (1:2), 20, 1871 (1:2).

5. *Ku Klux Conspiracy,* 7:943; *Biographical Souvenir of the States of Georgia and Florida: Containing the Sketches of Representative Public and Many Early Settled Families in These States* (1889; rpt. Easley, S. C.: Southern Historical Press, 1975), p. 729; U.S. Department of Commerce, Bureau of the Census, Fifth Census (1830) and Sixth Census (1840), Population, Pike County, Georgia.

6. *Ku Klux Conspiracy,* 7:938, 941.

7. *Savannah Morning News,* August 19, 1871 (4:1).

8. *Savannah Morning News,* August 31, 1871 (3:1); *Ku Klux Conspiracy,* 7:934–35.

9. *Ku Klux Conspiracy,* 7:846–47, 849.

10. Ibid., p. 848; *Washington New Era,* October 26, 1871 (3:1).

11. *Ku Klux Conspiracy,* 7:856; Tunis G. Campbell, *Sufferings of the Rev. T. G. Campbell and His Family in Georgia* (Washington, D.C.: Enterprise, 1877), p. 14.

12. Numan V. Bartley, *The Creation of Modern Georgia* (Athens: University of Georgia Press, 1983), pp. 70–71; Alan Conway, *The Reconstruction of Georgia* (Minneapolis: University of Minnesota Press, 1966), pp. 201–2; Charles E. Wynes, "The Politics of Reconstruction, Redemption, and Bourbonism," in Kenneth Coleman, ed., *A History of Georgia* (Athens: University of Georgia Press, 1977), p. 215.

13. *Acts and Resolutions of the General Assembly of Georgia, 1871* (Atlanta: W. A. Hemphill, 1872), pp. 265–66.

14. Ibid., pp. 265, 307; Benjamin Conley to Tunis Campbell, Tunis Campbell file.

15. A. W. Corker to Columbus Heard, May 20, 1872, Tunis Campbell file; *Savannah Daily Republican,* January 11, 1872 (2:2); Affidavits of Samuel Ross and Toby Maxwell, Tunis Campbell file.

16. *Journal of the Senate of the State of Georgia, 1872* (Atlanta: W. A. Hemphill, 1872), p. 46; *Savannah Daily Republican,* January 11, 1872 (2:2).

17. *Journal of the Senate of Georgia, 1872,* pp. 47, 65, 523; W. R. Gignilliat to R. E. Lester, January 1872, Tunis Campbell file.

18. "Witnesses For or Against Campbell" and "Petition," May 20, 1872, both in Tunis Campbell file.

19. Affidavit of Samuel Ross, Tunis Campbell file.

20. Affidavits of Toby Maxwell, Remus Elliott, Allen C. Gould, James Steel, Nero West, James Patterson, Lectured Crawford, Samuel Ross, ibid.

21. "Witnesses," Tunis Campbell file; Coulter, "Campbell," pp. 19, 29; Petition of McIntosh County Colored Citizens to U. S. Grant, August 10, 1875, Letters Received by the Department of Justice from the State of Georgia, 1871–1884, Record Group 60,

National Archives, Washington, D.C., Microcopy 996, Roll 2, p. 636, charges Lewis Jackson, Hamilton Jackson, and Alonzo Guyton with being "tools" of the white commissioners in exchange for public office.

22. Affidavit of W. R. Pritchard and J. Epping, Tunis Campbell file.

23. Affidavit of W. A. Burney, ibid.

24. Affidavit of E. E. Howard, ibid.

25. Lerone Bennett, *Black Power, USA: The Human Side of Reconstruction, 1867–1877* (Chicago: Johnson, 1967), p. 61; Frances Butler Leigh, *Ten Years on a Georgia Plantation since the War* (1883; rpt. New York: Negro Universities Press and Greenwood Publishing Corp., 1969), p. 135; Affidavit of Hamilton Jackson, Tunis Campbell file.

26. Affidavits of S. W. Wilson, A. W. Corker, and Hamilton Jackson, Tunis Campbell file; Leigh, *Ten Years on a Georgia Plantation*, pp. 37, 130–31, 137.

27. *Savannah Morning News,* January 11, 1872 (3:2); Affidavits of Hamilton Jackson, J. P. Gilson, and Ossian Hanks, Tunis Campbell file.

28. W.E.B. DuBois, "The Negro Landholder in Georgia," *Bulletin of the Department of Labor,* no. 35 (July 1901), pp. 651–53; Affidavits of W. A. Burney, W. R. Pritchard, J. Epping, George E. Atwood, A. W. Corker, and E. E. Howard; James H. Bradley to J. H. Taylor, June 13, 1870, Tunis Campbell file.

29. S. C. Williams to James M. Smith, April 1873, "Executive Department Correspondence," James M. Smith Papers, GDAH.

30. George S. Thomas to Edwards Pierrepont, August 7, 1875, Letters Received by the Department of Justice, Roll 2, p. 588.

31. Ibid., pp. 601–3; *Ku Klux Conspiracy,* 7:850, 858–59, 933–34; Coulter, "Campbell," p. 18.

32. *Ku Klux Conspiracy,* 7:858–59, 934; W. R. Gignilliat to R. E. Lester, January 1871, Tunis Campbell file; Thomas to Pierrepont, August 7, 1875, p. 603; T. G. Campbell to U. S. Grant, September 2, 1875, Letters Received by the Department of Justice, Roll 2, p. 734.

33. Thomas to Pierrepont, August 7, 1875, p. 588; *Reports of Cases in Law and Equity Argued and Determined in the Supreme Court of Georgia, at Atlanta, January 1873,* 235 vols. (Macon, Ga.: J. W. Burke, 1874), 48:357.

34. *Ku Klux Conspiracy,* 7:850, 858; Coulter, "Campbell," pp. 27–28.

35. Dorothy Sterling, ed., *The Trouble They Seen: Black People Tell the Story of Reconstruction* (Garden City, N.Y.: Doubleday, 1976), pp. 408, 410.

36. *Savannah Daily Republican,* January 13, 1872 (2:6); Paul L. Sanford, "The Negro in the Political Reconstruction of Georgia, 1865–1872" (M.A. thesis, Atlanta University, 1947), pp. 58–59.

37. *Atlanta Daily Sun,* August 9, 1872 (2:4); *Journal of the Senate of Georgia, 1872,* pp. 3, 291, 295.

38. *Atlanta Daily Sun,* August 17 (1:3, 2:4), 18, 1872 (2:4); *Atlanta Constitution,* August 17, 1872 (1:2); *Journal of the Senate of Georgia, 1872,* p. 367; Willard Range, *A Century of Georgia Agriculture, 1850–1950* (Athens: University of Georgia Press, 1954), p. 122; Sterling, *Trouble They Seen,* p. 350; I. W. Avery, *The History of the State of Georgia from 1850 to 1881, Embracing the Three Important Epochs: The Decade before the War of 1861–5; The War; The Period of Reconstruction* (New York: Brown & Derby, 1881), p. 503; W. Augustus Low and Virgil A. Clift, eds., *Encyclopedia of Black America* (New York: McGraw-Hill, 1981), p. 144.

39. *Journal of the Senate of Georgia, 1872,* pp. 522–34; Edward B. Young, "The Negro in Georgia Politics, 1867–1877" (M.S. thesis, Emory University, 1955), pp. 71–72; E. Merton Coulter, *Negro Legislators in Georgia during the Reconstruction Period* (Athens: University of Georgia Press, 1968), p. 156.

40. *Savannah Morning News,* September 18, 1872 (3:3).

41. T. G. Campbell to E. D. Morgan, July 8, 1872, as quoted in Coulter, "Campbell," p. 28; *Darien Timber Gazette,* October 6, 1876 (3:2).

42. "T. G. Campbell vs. H. W. Mattox," Contested Elections, Second District, 1872, GDAH; *Journal of the Senate of Georgia, 1873* (Macon, Ga.: J. W. Burke, 1874), p. 3.

43. *Report of Cases in Law and Equity, 1873,* p. 357.

44. *Ku Klux Conspiracy,* 7:858–59, 942.

45. *Journal of the Senate of Georgia, 1874* (Macon, Ga.: J. W. Burke, 1874), p. 67; "T. G. Campbell vs. H. W. Mattox."

46. McIntosh County, Superior Court Minutes, 1873–80, Microfilm, pp. 1–110; S. C. Williams to James M. Smith, April 1873, both in GDAH.

47. *Savannah Morning News,* June 28, 1872 (3:2). Archibald McKinley Diary, April 7, 1873, University of Georgia, Athens, Ga.; McIntosh County, Superior Court Minutes, pp. 28, 59, 89; McIntosh County, Tax Digests, 1871, and "Robert E. Carr vs. T. G. Campbell, Sr.," McIntosh County Records, State Court, both in GDAH.

48. The Republican split occurred while Bullock was in office. Led by the "Augusta Ring" of Henry P. Farrow, Foster Blodgett, and John E. Bryant, moderates often combined with Democrats to defeat Bullock's more radical proposals. See Olive Hall Shadgett, *The Republican Party in Georgia from Reconstruction through 1900* (Athens: University of Georgia Press, 1964), pp. 7–12; Ruth C. McDaniel, "Georgia Carpetbagger: John Emory Bryant and the Ambiguity of Reform during Reconstruction" (Ph.D. dissertation, Duke University, 1974), p. 183; U.S. Census Bureau, Ninth Census (1870), Population Schedule, Burke County, Georgia; *Savannah City Directory, 1874–1875* (Savannah: J. H. Estill, 1874).

49. *Savannah Morning News,* September 17 (3:4), 24 (3:3), October 3 (3:3), 20, 1874 (3:3); *Darien Timber Gazette,* September 19 (2:1), October 10 (3:2), 31 (2:3), November 7, 1874 (3:3); *Annual Report of the Comptroller General of the State of Georgia for the Year 1874* (Savannah: J. H. Estill, 1875), p. 52.

50. *Darien Timber Gazette,* October 3, (3:1, 3:3), 31 (2:3), November 14, 1874 (3:3).

51. Ibid., October 10, 1874 (3:2); Albert Colbey Smith, "Down Freedom's Road: The Contours of Race, Class, and Property Crime in Black-Belt Georgia, 1866–1910" (Ph.D. dissertation, University of Georgia, 1982), p. 220; interview with Mrs. R. E. Gill (John Fisher's granddaughter), Darien, Ga., May 10, 1984.

52. Coulter, "Campbell," p. 35; Petition of McIntosh Citizens to U. S. Grant, June 1, 1875, Letters Received by the Department of Justice, Roll 2, pp. 625–26; Henry M. Turner to the editor of the *Savannah Journal,* undated, in *Washington New National Era* July 11, 1872, as quoted in Sterling, ed., *Trouble They Seen,* pp. 408–9.

53. McIntosh County, Superior Court Minutes, p. 128; Campbell, *Sufferings,* pp. 15–16; *Savannah Morning News,* January 21, 1875 (3:3).

54. McIntosh County, Superior Court Minutes, p. 128; Smith, "Down Freedom's Road," pp. 126–27; Thomas to Pierrepont, Au-

gust 7, 1875, p. 586; *Darien Timber Gazette,* January 16, 1875 (3:1); T. G. Campbell to U. S. Grant, September 2, 1875, Letters Received by the Department of Justice, Roll 2, p. 739.

55. Thomas to Pierrepont, August 7, 1875, pp. 582–83; Campbell, *Sufferings,* p. 16; McIntosh County, Superior Court Minutes, pp. 128, 134; *Darien Timber Gazette,* January 16, 1875 (3:1); *Savannah Morning News,* January 12, 1876 (3:4); "State vs. Tunis Campbell," McIntosh County Records, Superior Court, GDAH.

56. Thomas to Pierrepont, August 7, 1875, pp. 581–85; *Darien Timber Gazette,* January 16, 1875 (3:1); Campbell, *Sufferings,* p. 17; *Savannah Morning News,* January 12, 1876 (3:4), January 12, 1875 (3:5).

57. Coulter, "Campbell," p. 36; *Darien Timber Gazette,* January 16, 1875 (3:1).

58. Coulter, "Campbell," p. 37; Thomas to Pierrepont, August 7, 1875, p. 589.

59. *Savannah Morning News,* January 21, 1875 (3:3–4); *Atlanta Constitution,* January 16, 1875 (3:5).

60. Campbell, *Sufferings,* pp. 18–19; Thomas to Pierrepont, August 7, 1875, p. 589; *Atlanta Constitution,* January 24, 1875 (3:5); *Savannah Morning News,* February 5, 1875 (3:4); *Darien Timber Gazette,* January 23 (3:3), 30, 1875 (3:4).

61. T. G. Campbell to U. S. Grant, September 7, 1875, Letters Received by the Department of Justice, Roll 2, pp. 735–36; *Journal of the Georgia House of Representatives, 1875* (Savannah: J. H. Estill, 1875), pp. 291, 318.

62. Coulter, "Campbell," pp. 34–35, 39; *Journal of the Georgia House, 1875,* p. 398.

63. Campbell, *Sufferings,* p. 22.

64. Thomas to Pierrepont, August 7, 1875, pp. 581, 585–87, 589–92, 601; McIntosh County, Superior Court Minutes, p. 151.

65. Thomas to Pierrepont, August 7, 1875, p. 590; *Darien Timber Gazette,* May 1 (3:3), 8, 1875 (3:2); McIntosh County, Superior Court Minutes, p. 159.

66. *Darien Timber Gazette,* May 8, 1875 (3:2), October 6, 1876 (3:2–3); McKinley Diary, April 30, 1875; Colored Citizens to U. S. Grant, August 10, 1875, Letters Received by the Department of Justice, Roll 2, p. 628.

67. McKinley Diary, May 1, 1875; *Darien Timber Gazette,* May 8 (3:2), 28, 1875 (3:2), October 6, 1876 (3:3); Betsy Fancher, *The Lost Legacy of Georgia's Golden Isles* (Garden City, N.Y.: Doubleday, 1971), p. 140.

68. T. G. Campbell to U. S. Grant, September 2, 1875, 734–41; U. S. Grant to H. P. Farrow, November 19, 1875, Letters Received by the Department of Justice, Roll 1, p. 40; Thomas to Pierrepont, August 7, 1875, pp. 576, 598–99; Petition to U. S. Grant, June 1, 1875, Letters Received by the Department of Justice, Roll 2, pp. 625–27.

69. Colored Citizens to U. S. Grant, August 10, 1875, p. 633; Joseph Hilton and W. C. Clarke to James M. Smith, November 24, 1875, "Executive Dept. Correspondence," James M. Smith Papers, GDAH.

70. C. B. Clark to U. S. Grant, June 24, 1875, Letters Received by the Department of Justice, Roll 2, pp. 543–44; C. B. Clark to T. S. Phillips, July 7, 1875, ibid.; *U.S. City Directories,* Buffalo, New York, 1876, Microfilm, pp. 325–26, 694.

71. George S. Thomas to Edwards Pierrepont, August 2, 1875, Letters Received by the Department of Justice, Roll 2, pp. 571, 577, 579–82, 586–87; *Savannah Colored Tribune,* January 15 (3:2), 22, 1876 (2:1); *Savannah Morning News,* November 15, 1875 (3:4).

72. Henry P. Farrow to Edwards Pierrepont, November 30, 1875, Letters Received by the Department of Justice, Roll 2, pp. 779–81; *Darien Timber Gazette,* December 3, 1875 (3:4); *Savannah Morning News,* November 29, 1875 (3:5).

73. Henry P. Farrow to Edwards Pierrepont, December 13, 1875, Letters Received by the Department of Justice, Roll 2, pp. 789–90; McIntosh County, Superior Court Minutes, pp. 243–44, 248–49; *Savannah Colored Tribune,* January 15, 1876 (3:2); McIntosh County Records, "Treasury 1873–1879," GDAH.

74. Department of Corrections, Account Book of Convicts Leased 1872–76; Department of Corrections, Register of Convicts at Individual Camps, Miscellaneous Camps, and Lessees 1871–81, both in GDAH; *Darien Timber Gazette,* January 28 (3:3), February 4 (3:1), July 21 (3:1), August 11, 1876 (3:3); Campbell, *Sufferings,* pp. 25–26.

75. *Savannah Colored Tribune,* May 13 (1:3), 20, 1876 (1:2).

76. Department of Corrections, Registers of Convicts Received,

Pardoned, Discharged, Died, or Escaped, 1871–86, GDAH; *Darien Timber Gazette,* January 26, 1877 (3:3); Campbell, *Sufferings,* p. 3; *Washington Evening Star,* June 8, 1877 (4:2); *U.S. City Directories,* Washington, D.C., 1878.

EPILOGUE

1. Albert Colbey Smith, "Down Freedom's Road: The Contours of Race, Class, and Property Crime in Black-Belt Georgia, 1866–1915" (Ph.D. dissertation, University of Georgia, 1982), p. 128.

2. Ibid., pp. 132, 151.

3. E. Merton Coulter, "Tunis G. Campbell: Negro Reconstructionist in Georgia," *Georgia Historical Quarterly* 52 (March 1968):46–47; *Darien Timber Gazette,* May 26 (3:3), June 9 (3:2–3), July 29, 1882 (3:2).

4. *Darien Timber Gazette,* August 12 (3:1), September 16, 1882 (3:1); *Savannah Morning News,* August 3, 1882 (1:5); *Atlanta Constitution,* August 3, 1882 (4:1).

5. *Darien Timber Gazette,* June 9 (3:4), July 29 (3:2), August 5, 1882 (3:1).

6. Ibid., August 26 (3:1,4), September 16 (3:1), November 11, 1882 (3:4).

7. Ibid., January 6, 1882 (3:1); *U.S. City Directories, 1882–1901,* Boston, Massachusetts, Microfilm, Reel 9, 1892, p. 234; *Boston Morning Journal,* December 5, 1891 (3:2).

8. See Coulter, "Campbell," for a prejudicial view of Campbell's efforts among Georgia's freedmen.

SELECTED BIBLIOGRAPHY

PRIMARY SOURCES

Manuscripts

ATHENS, GEORGIA
University of Georgia Library.
William Cooke Plantation Book, 1861–67.
Archibald McKinley Diary.
U.S. Department of Commerce. Bureau of the Census. Manuscript Agricultural Schedules. McIntosh County, Georgia, 1880. Microfilm.
———. Population Schedules. Liberty County, Georgia, 1850 and 1860. Microfilm.
———. Population Schedules. McIntosh County, Georgia, 1850–1870. Microfilm.
———. Slave Schedules. Liberty County, Georgia, 1850 and 1860. Microfilm.
———. Slave Schedules. McIntosh County, Georgia, 1850 and 1860. Microfilm.
George Wagner Papers.
Robert E. Williams Photographic Archive.
William E. Wilson Photographic Archive.

ATLANTA, GEORGIA
Atlanta Historical Society.
Benjamin F. Conley Papers.
Georgia Department of Archives and History.
Tunis Campbell file.
Contested Elections. Second District, 1872. "T. G. Campbell vs. H. W. Mattox."

Department of Corrections. Account Book of Convicts Leased, 1872–76.

———. Inmate Administration Division. Central Register of Convicts, 1866–79. Vol. 3.

———. Register of Convicts at Individual Camps, Miscellaneous Camps, and Lessees, 1871–81.

———. Registers of Convicts Received, Pardoned, Discharged, Died or Escaped, 1871–86.

McIntosh County. Board of Education Minutes, 1873–86.

———. City Court Records. "McIntosh County and Her Resources."

———. Court of Ordinary, Minutes, 1873–86.

———. Superior Court Minutes, 1873–80.

———. Tax Digests, 1871–79.

McIntosh County Academy, 1820–1903.

McIntosh County file.

McIntosh County Records. Grand Jury Presentments, 1872–77.

———. State Court. "Robert E. Carr vs. T. G. Campbell, Sr."

———. Superior Court.

———. Treasury, 1873–79.

Negroes file.

Reconstruction file.

Reconstruction Registration Oath Books. District 2. McIntosh County.

Reconstruction Registration Record. District 2. McIntosh County.

James M. Smith Papers.

DARIEN, GEORGIA

Court of the Ordinary. "Record of Wills: May 1873–November 1915."

Darien City Hall. Minutes of the Port of Darien, Board of Pilot Commissioners.

Office of the Board of Education. Minutes of the Board of Commissioners, 1875–82.

NEW ORLEANS, LOUISIANA

Amistad Research Center, Dillard University. American Missionary Association Manuscripts, Letters from Georgia. Microfilm.

SAVANNAH, GEORGIA

Georgia Historical Society.

Uncatalogued MSS Collection No. 2031. Freedmen's Bureau Records. "BelleVille."

————. "McIntosh County."

————. "St. Catherine's Island."

Hilton Papers.

Bessie Lewis Papers.

WASHINGTON, D.C.

National Archives.

Record Group 56. Consolidated Index of Claims Reported by the Commissioners of Claims to the House of Representatives from 1871 to 1880. Microcopy 87. Rolls 13 and 14.

Record Group 60. Letters Received by the Department of Justice from the State of Georgia, 1871–84. Microcopy 996.

Record Group 105. Bureau of Refugees, Freedmen, and Abandoned Lands, Georgia. Records of the Assistant Commissioner. Microcopy 798.

————. Bureau of Refugees, Freedmen, and Abandoned Lands, Records of the Assistant Commissioner for the State of South Carolina. Microcopy 869.

————. Bureau of Refugees, Freedmen, and Abandoned Lands, Records of the Surgeon-in-Chief for the State of Georgia, 1865–68.

————. Bureau of Refugees, Freedmen, and Abandoned Lands, Washington, D.C. Headquarters. Registers and Letters Received by the Commissioner. Microcopy 752.

————. Records of the Education Division of the Bureau of Refugees, Freedmen, and Abandoned Lands, 1865–71. Microcopy 803.

Newspapers and Periodicals

American Missionary (New York).

Atlanta Constitution.

Atlanta Daily New Era.

Atlanta Daily Sun.

Augusta (Ga.) *Daily Loyal Georgian.*

Augusta (Ga.) *Weekly Constitutionalist.*
Augusta (Ga.) *Weekly Loyal Georgian.*
Darien (Ga.) *Timber Gazette.*
Frederick Douglass' Paper (Rochester, N.Y.).
Rochester North Star.
Savannah Colored Tribune.
Savannah Daily Herald.
Savannah Daily Republican.
Savannah Morning News.

Published Sources

Abrams, Alexander St. Clair. *Manual and Biographical Register of
the State of Georgia, 1871–2.* Atlanta: Plantation Press, 1872.
Alvord, J. W. "Letters from the South Relating to the Condition of
the Freedmen." Washington, D.C.: Howard University Press,
1870.
Andrews, Sidney. *The South since the War, as Shown by the Four-
teen Weeks of Travel and Observation in Georgia and the Car-
olinas.* 1866. Reprint. Boston: Houghton Mifflin, 1971.
Campbell, Tunis G. *Hotel Keepers, Head Waiters, and Housekeepers'
Guide.* Boston: Coolidge and Wiley, 1848. Reprint. *Never Let Peo-
ple Be Kept Waiting: A Textbook on Hotel Management.* Edited by
Doris Elizabeth King. Raleigh, N.C.: Graphic Press, 1973.
———. *Sufferings of the Rev. T. G. Campbell and His Family in
Georgia.* Washington, D.C.: Enterprise, 1877.
*Can a Negro Hold Office in Georgia?: Decided in the Supreme Court
of Georgia, June Term, 1869.* Atlanta: Daily Intelligencer Book
and Job Office, 1869.
Candler, Allen D., ed. *The Confederate Records of the State of Geor-
gia.* 5 vols. Atlanta: State Printer, 1910.
Conrad, Georgia Bryan. *Reminiscences of a Southern Woman.*
Hampton, Va.: Hampton Institute Press, 1901.
Fleming, Walter L., ed. *Documentary History of Reconstruction: Po-
litical, Military, Social, Religious, Educational, and Industrial,
1865 to 1906.* 1907. Reprint. 2 vols. New York: McGraw-Hill,
1966.
Georgia. Comptroller General's Office. *Report of Madison Bell,*

Comptroller General of the State of Georgia, Covering the Period from August 11, 1868 to January 1, 1869. Atlanta: Samuel Bard, Public Printer, 1869.

Georgia. Constitutional Convention. *Constitution, Ordinances, and Resolutions of the Georgia Convention Assembled in Pursuance of the Reconstruction Acts of Congress and Held by Order of General Pope in the City of Atlanta in 1867 and 1868.* Atlanta: New Era Office, 1868.

————. *Journal of the Proceedings of the Constitutional Convention of the People of Georgia Held in the City of Atlanta in the Months of December, 1867, and January, February, and March, 1868.* Augusta: E. H. Pughe, 1868.

Georgia. Department of Agriculture. *First Annual Report of the Commissioner of Agriculture, Being for the Year 1874.* Savannah: J. H. Estill, Public Printer, 1875.

Georgia. General Assembly. House. *Journal of the House of Representatives of the State of Georgia.* Places and publishers vary, 1868–75.

Georgia. General Assembly. Senate. *Journal of the Senate of the State of Georgia, 1868–1876.* Places and publishers vary, 1868–76.

Georgia. Penitentiary. *Biennial Report of the Principal Keeper of the Georgia Penitentiary from the 1st of January, 1877 to the 20th of October, 1878.* Atlanta: James Harrison, n.d.

————. *Report of the Principal Keeper of the Georgia Penitentiary, from the 1st day of January, 1876, to the 31st of December, 1876.* Atlanta: H. G. Wright, 1877.

Georgia. Statutes, Laws, etc. *Acts and Resolutions of the General Assembly of Georgia, 1871.* Atlanta: W. A. Hemphill, 1872.

Georgia. Supreme Court. 253 vols. *Reports of Cases in Law and Equity Argued and Determined in the Supreme Court of Georgia, at Atlanta, January 1873.* Vol. 48. Macon, Ga.: J. W. Burke, 1874.

Grant, U. S. "An Act to Promote the Reconstruction of Georgia." Washington, D.C.: U.S. Government Printing Office, 1870.

Holmes, James. *"Dr. Bullie's" Notes: Reminiscences of Early Georgia and of Philadelphia and New Haven in the 1800's.* 1880. Reprint. Edited by Delma Eugene Presley. Atlanta: Cherokee, 1976.

Howard, Oliver Otis. *Autobiography of Oliver Otis Howard, Major General United States Army.* 2 vols. New York: Baker & Taylor, 1907.

Kemble, Frances Anne. *Journal of a Residence on a Georgian Plantation in 1838–1839.* 1863. Reprint. Edited by John A. Scott. Athens: University of Georgia Press, 1984.

Leigh, Frances Butler. *Ten Years on a Georgia Plantation since the War.* 1883. Reprint. New York: Negro Universities Press, Greenwood Publishing Corp., 1969.

Leigh, J. W. *Other Days.* New York: Macmillan, 1921.

McPherson, Edward, ed. *The Political History of the United States of America during the Period of Reconstruction.* Washington, D.C.: Solomons & Chapman, 1875.

Nordhoff, Charles. *The Cotton States in the Spring and Summer of 1875.* New York: D. Appleton, 1876.

Rawick, George P., ed. *The American Slave: A Composite Autobiography.* Vols. 12 and 13: *Georgia Narratives.* Westport, Conn.: Greenwood, 1972.

Saxton, Rufus. *General Orders, etc., Issued by Maj.-Gen. Rufus Saxton, as Military Governor, Department of the South and as Asst. Commissioner BRFAL of South Carolina, Georgia, and Florida, 1862–1866.* Washington, D.C.: n.p., 1867.

Savannah City Directories, 1867–1880. Savannah: J. H. Estill, dates vary.

Schurz, Carl. *Report on the Condition of the South.* New York: New York Times & Arno Press, 1969.

Sherman, William T. *Memoirs of Gen. W. T. Sherman.* 2 vols. New York: Charles L. Webster, 1891.

Sterling, Dorothy, ed. *The Trouble They Seen: Black People Tell the Story of Reconstruction.* Garden City, N.Y.: Doubleday, 1976.

Taylor, Susie K. *Reminiscences of My Life in Camp with the 33d United States Colored Troops, Late 1st S.C. Volunteers.* 1902. Reprint. New York: Arno Press, 1968.

Thomas, Edward J. *Memoirs of a Southerner, 1840–1923.* Savannah: By the author, 1923.

U.S. Congress. *House Miscellaneous Documents.* 40th Cong., 3d sess., No. 52. Parts 1 and 2 (serial 1385).

──────. *Report of the Joint Committee on Reconstruction.* 39th Cong., 1st sess., House Report 30 (serial 1273).

———. *Report of the Joint Select Committee to Inquire into the Condition of Affairs in the Late Insurrectionary States.* 13 vols. Washington, D.C.: U.S. Government Printing Office, 1872.

———. *Senate Executive Documents.* 39th Cong., 1st sess., Part 1, No. 2 (serial 1237).

———. *Senate Executive Documents.* 39th Cong., 1st sess., Part 2, No. 27 (serial 1238).

———. *Senate Executive Documents.* 39th Cong., 2d sess., No. 6 (serial 1276).

———. *Senate Executive Documents.* 40th Cong., 1st sess., No. 14, (serial 1308).

———. *Senate Executive Documents.* 41st Cong., 2d sess., No. 41, (serial 1406).

U.S. Department of Agriculture. *Report of the Commissioner of Agriculture for the Years 1866–1880.* 15 vols. Washington, D.C.: U.S. Government Printing Office, 1866–80.

U.S. Department of Commerce. *Negro Population, 1790–1915.* Washington, D.C.: U.S. Government Printing Office, 1918.

———. *Ninth Census of the United States, 1870: Statistics of Population.* Washington, D.C.: U.S. Government Printing Office, 1872.

War of the Rebellion: A Compilation of the Official Records of the Union and Confederate Armies. 128 vols. Washington, D.C.: U.S. Government Printing Office, 1880–1901.

Wylly, Charles Spalding. *Memories and Annals.* Brunswick, Ga.: Glover Bros., 1916.

SECONDARY SOURCES

Allen, James S. *The Negro Question in the United States.* New York: International Publishers, 1936.

———. *Reconstruction: The Battle for Democracy, 1865–1876.* New York: International Publishers, 1937.

Alston, L. J., and Higgs, Robert. "Contractual Mix in Southern Agriculture since the Civil War: Facts. Hypotheses, and Tests." *Journal of Economic History* 42 (June 1982):327–53.

Armstrong, Margaret N. *Fanny Kemble: A Passionate Victorian.* New York: Macmillan, 1938.

Armstrong, Thomas F. "From Task Labor to Free Labor: The Transition along Georgia's Rice Coast, 1820–1880." *Georgia Historical Quarterly* 54 (Winter 1980):432–47.

Avery, I. W. *The History of the State of Georgia from 1850 to 1881, Embracing the Three Important Epochs: The Decade before the War of 1861–5; The War; The Period of Reconstruction.* New York: Brown & Derby, 1881.

Bacote, Clarence A. "The Negro in Georgia Politics, 1880–1908." Ph.D. dissertation, University of Chicago, 1955.

Banks, Enoch M. *The Economics of Land Tenure in Georgia.* New York: Columbia University Press, 1905.

Bartley, Numan V. *The Creation of Modern Georgia.* Athens: University of Georgia Press, 1983.

Baughman, Laurence E. *Southern Rape Complex: Hundred Year Psychosis.* Atlanta: Pendulum Books, 1966.

Beale, Howard K. "On Rewriting Reconstruction History." *American Historical Review* 45 (July 1940):807–27.

Bennett, Lerone. *Black Power, USA: The Human Side of Reconstruction, 1867–1877.* Chicago: Johnson, 1967.

Bentley, George R. *A History of the Freedmen's Bureau.* Philadelphia: University of Pennsylvania Press, 1955.

Billings, Dwight B., Jr. *Planters and the Making of a "New South": Class, Politics, and Development in North Carolina, 1865–1900.* Chapel Hill: University of North Carolina Press, 1979.

Bloom, Charles G. "The Georgia Election of April, 1868: A Re-Examination of the Politics of Georgia Reconstruction." M.A. thesis, University of Chicago, 1963.

Bonner, James C. *The Georgia Story.* Oklahoma City: Harlow, 1958.

Botkin, Benjamin A., ed. *Lay My Burden Down: A Folk History of Slavery.* Chicago: University of Chicago Press, 1945.

Brooks, Robert Preston. *The Agrarian Revolution in Georgia, 1865–1912.* Madison: University of Wisconsin Press, 1914.

Busbee, Westley, F., Jr. "Presidential Reconstruction in Georgia, 1865–1867." Ph.D. dissertation, University of Alabama, 1973.

Carson, Robert F. "The Loyal League in Georgia." *Georgia Historical Quarterly* 20 (June 1936):125–53.

Cash, Wilbur J. *The Mind of the South.* 1941. Reprint. New York: Alfred A. Knopf, 1969.

Cate, Margaret Davis. *Early Days of Coastal Georgia.* St. Simons Island, Ga.: Fort Frederica Association, 1955.

Cheney, Brainard. *River Rogue.* 1942. Reprint. Washington, D.C.: Burr Oak Publishers, 1982.

Christler, Ethel M. "Participation of Negroes in the Government of Georgia, 1867–1870." M.A. thesis, Atlanta University, 1932.

Cimbala, Paul. "The Terms of Freedom: The Freedmen's Bureau and Reconstruction in Georgia, 1865–1870." Ph.D. dissertation, Emory University, 1983.

Clifton, James. "Twilight Comes to the Rice Kingdom: Postbellum Rice Culture on the South Atlantic Coast." *Georgia Historical Quarterly* 62 (Summer 1978):146–54.

Coleman, Kenneth, and Gurr, Charles Stephen, eds. *Dictionary of Georgia Biography.* 2 vols. Athens: University of Georgia Press, 1983.

Conway, Alan. *The Reconstruction of Georgia.* Minneapolis: University of Minnesota Press, 1966.

Cook, Jim. Ardock, Ga. Interview, May 16, 1984.

Coulter, E. Merton. *Negro Legislators in Georgia during the Reconstruction Period.* Athens: University of Georgia Press, 1968.

———. "Robert Gould Shaw and the Burning of Darien." *Civil War History* 5 (December 1959):363–73.

———. "Tunis G. Campbell, Negro Reconstructionist in Georgia." *Georgia Historical Quarterly* 51 (December 1967):401–24; 52 (March 1968):16–52.

Current, Richard N. "Carpetbaggers Reconsidered." In David Pinkney and Theodore Ropp, eds., *A Festschrift for Frederick B. Artz.* Durham: Duke University Press, 1964.

DeCanio, Stephen J. *Agriculture in the Postbellum South: The Economics of Production and Supply.* Cambridge, Mass.: MIT Press, 1974.

Drago, Edmund L. *Black Politicians and Reconstruction in Georgia: A Splendid Failure.* Baton Rouge: Louisiana State University Press, 1982.

———. "Militancy and Black Women in Reconstruction Georgia." *Journal of American Culture* 1 (Winter 1978):838–44.

Drake, Richard Bryant. "The American Missionary Association and the Southern Negro, 1861–1888." Ph.D. dissertation, Emory University, 1957.

Drake, Samuel A. *Georgia: Its History, Condition, and Resources.* New York: Charles Scribner's Sons, 1879.

DuBois, W.E.B. *Black Reconstruction in America: An Essay toward a History of the Part Which Black Folk Played in the Attempt to Reconstruct Democracy in America, 1860–1880.* New York: Atheneum, 1979.

———. "The Negro Landholder in Georgia." *Bulletin of the Department of Labor,* no. 35 (July 1901), pp. 647–77.

———. *The Souls of Black Folk: Essays and Sketches.* Greenwich, Conn.: Fawcett Press, 1964.

Duncan, Russell. "From Black-Separatism to Black Power: Tunis Campbell and the Black Majority in Coastal Georgia during Reconstruction." M.A. thesis, University of Georgia, 1984.

Engerrand, Steven W. " 'Now Scratch or Die': The Genesis of Capitalistic Agricultural Labor in Georgia, 1865–1880." Ph.D. dissertation, University of Georgia, 1981.

Escott, Paul D. *Slavery Remembered: A Record of Twentieth Century Slave Narratives.* Chapel Hill: University of North Carolina Press, 1979.

Fancher, Betsy. *The Lost Legacy of Georgia's Golden Isles.* Garden City, N.Y.: Doubleday, 1971.

Fields, Barbara J. "Ideology and Race in American History." In J. Morgan Kousser and James M. McPherson, eds., *Region, Race, and Reconstruction: Essays in Honor of C. Vann Woodward,* pp. 143–77. New York: Oxford University Press, 1982.

Fitz-Simons, Theodore Baker, Jr. "The Ku Klux Klan in Georgia, 1868–1871." M.A. thesis, University of Georgia, 1957.

Flynn, Charles L., Jr. *White Land, Black Labor: Caste and Class in Late Nineteenth-Century Georgia.* Baton Rouge: Louisiana State University Press, 1983.

Foner, Eric. *Nothing But Freedom: Emancipation and Its Legacy.* Baton Rouge: Louisiana State University Press, 1983.

———. "Reconstruction Revisited." *Reviews in American History* 10 (December 1982):82–100.

Franklin, John Hope. *From Slavery to Freedom: A History of Negro Americans.* 5th ed. New York: Alfred A. Knopf, 1980.

———. *Reconstruction: After the Civil War.* Chicago: University of Chicago Press, 1961.

Genovese, Eugene D. *The Political Economy of Slavery: Studies in the Economy and Society of the Slave South.* New York: Pantheon Books, 1965.

Gerteis, Louis S. *From Contraband to Freedom: Federal Policy toward Southern Blacks, 1861–1865.* Westport, Conn.: Greenwood Press, 1973.

Gill, Mrs. R. E. Darien, Ga. Interview. May 10, 1984.

Gottlieb, Manuel. "The Land Question in Georgia during Reconstruction." *Science and Society* 3 (1939):356–88.

Gordon, Asa H. *The Georgia Negro: A History.* 1937. Reprint. Spartanburg, S.C.: Reprint Co., 1972.

Gutman, Herbert G. *The Black Family in Slavery and Freedom, 1750–1925.* New York: Pantheon Books, 1976.

Hall, Raymond L. *Black Separatism in the United States.* Hanover, N.H.: University Press of New England, 1978.

Harper, Roland M. "Agriculture in Lower Georgia, 1850–1880." *Georgia Historical Quarterly* 6 (June 1922):95–121.

Harris, William. *The Harder We Run: Black Workers since the Civil War.* New York: Oxford University Press, 1982.

Hermann, Janet Sharp. *The Pursuit of a Dream.* New York: Oxford University Press, 1981.

Higgs, Robert. *Competition and Coercion: Blacks in the American Economy, 1865–1914.* Cambridge: Cambridge University Press, 1977.

Hoffman, Edwin D. "From Slavery to Self-Reliance: The Record of Achievement of the Freedmen of the Sea Island Region." *Journal of Negro History* 41 (January 1956):8–42.

Hollingsworth, R. R. "Education and Reconstruction in Georgia." *Georgia Historical Quarterly* 19 (June 1935):112–33; 20 (September 1935):229–50.

Holt, Thomas. *Black over White: Negro Political Leaders in South Carolina during Reconstruction.* Urbana: University of Illinois Press, 1977.

House, A. V., Jr. "Reconstruction Share-Cropper Contract on a Georgia Rice Plantation." *Georgia Historical Quarterly* 26 (June 1942):156–65.

Jones, Jacqueline. *Soldiers of Light and Love: Northern Teachers and Georgia Blacks, 1865–1873.* Chapel Hill: University of North Carolina Press, 1980.

King, Spencer Bidwell. *Darien: The Death and Rebirth of a Southern Town*. Macon, Ga.: Mercer University Press, 1981.

Lawe, Theodore Maxwell. "The Black Reconstructionist in Georgia: 1865–1877." M.A. thesis, Atlanta University, 1966.

Levine, Lawrence W. *Black Culture and Black Consciousness: Afro-American Folk Thought from Slavery to Freedom*. New York: Oxford University Press, 1978.

Lewis, Bessie. *They Called Their Town Darien: Being a Short History of Darien and McIntosh County, Georgia*. Darien, Ga.: Darien News, 1975.

Litwack, Leon F. *Been in the Storm So Long: The Aftermath of Slavery*. New York: Alfred A. Knopf, 1979.

Lovell, Caroline Couper. *The Golden Isles of Georgia*. Boston: Little, Brown, 1932.

Low, W. Augustus, and Clift, Virgil A., eds. *Encyclopedia of Black America*. New York: McGraw-Hill, 1981.

McFeely, William S. *Yankee Stepfather: General O. O. Howard and the Freedmen*. New Haven: Yale University Press, 1968.

McPherson, James M. *Ordeal by Fire: The Civil War and Reconstruction*. New York: Alfred A. Knopf, 1982.

Magdol, Edward. *A Right to the Land: Essays on the Freedmen's Community*. Westport, Conn.: Greenwood Press, 1977.

Mandle, Jay. *The Roots of Black Poverty: The Southern Plantation Economy after the Civil War*. Durham: Duke University Press, 1978.

Matthews, John M. "The Negro in Georgia Politics, 1865–1880." M.A. thesis, Duke University, 1967.

————. "Negro Republicans in the Reconstruction of Georgia." *Georgia Historical Quarterly* 60 (Summer 1976):145–64.

Mitchell, Margaret. *Gone With the Wind*. 1936. Reprint. New York: Macmillan, 1964.

Mohr, Clarence M. "Before Sherman: Georgia Blacks and the Union War Effort." *Journal of Southern History* 45 (August 1979):331–53.

————. "Georgia Blacks during Secession and Civil War, 1859–1865." Ph.D. dissertation, University of Georgia, 1975.

Morrison, Carlton A. "Raftsmen of the Altamaha." M.A. thesis, University of Georgia, 1970.

Nathans, Elizabeth Studley. *Losing the Peace: Georgia Republicans and Reconstruction, 1865–1871.* Baton Rouge: Louisiana State University Press, 1968.

Oubre, Claude F. *Forty Acres and a Mule: The Freedmen's Bureau and Black Land Ownership.* Baton Rouge: Louisiana State University Press, 1978.

Owens, James Leggette. "The Negro in Georgia during Reconstruction, 1864–1872: A Social History." Ph.D. dissertation, University of Georgia, 1975.

Patrick, Rembert W. *The Reconstruction of the Nation.* New York: Oxford University Press, 1967.

Peirce, Paul S. *The Freedmen's Bureau: A Chapter in the History of Reconstruction.* State University of Iowa Studies in Sociology, Economics, Politics, and History, vol. 3, no. 1. Iowa City: State University of Iowa, 1904.

Perdue, Robert E. *The Negro in Savannah, 1865–1900.* New York: Exposition Press, 1973.

Powell, L. N. *New Masters: Northern Planters during the Civil War and Reconstruction.* New Haven: Yale University Press, 1980.

Pressly, Thomas J., and Scofield, William H., eds. *Farm Real Estate Values in the United States by Counties, 1850–1959.* Seattle: University of Washington Press, 1965.

Rabinowitz, Howard N. *Race Relations in the Urban South, 1865–1890.* New York: Oxford University Press, 1978.

————, ed. *Southern Black Leaders of the Reconstruction Era.* Urbana: University of Illinois Press, 1982.

Range, Willard. *A Century of Georgia Agriculture, 1850–1950.* Athens: University of Georgia Press, 1954.

Ransom, Roger L., and Sutch, Richard. *One Kind of Freedom: The Economic Consequences of Emancipation.* Cambridge: Cambridge University Press, 1977.

Roark, James L. *Masters without Slaves: Southern Planters in the Civil War and Reconstruction.* New York: Norton, 1977.

Robinson, Armistead. "Beyond the Realm of Social Consciousness: New Meanings of Reconstruction for American History." *Journal of American History* 68 (May 1981):276–97.

Rogers, George A., and Saunders, R. Frank. *Swamp Water and Wiregrass: Historical Sketches of Coastal Georgia.* Macon, Ga.: Mercer University Press, 1984.

Sanford, Paul Laurence. "The Negro in the Political Reconstruction of Georgia, 1865–1872." M.A. thesis, Atlanta University, 1947.

Scroggs, Jack B. "Carpetbagger Influence in the Political Reconstruction of the South Atlantic States, 1865–1876." Ph.D. dissertation, University of North Carolina, 1951.

Sefton, James E. *The United States Army and Reconstruction, 1865–1877*. Baton Rouge: Louisiana State University Press, 1967.

Shadgett, Olive Hall. *The Republican Party in Georgia from Reconstruction through 1900*. Athens: University of Georgia Press, 1964.

Simkins, Francis B. "New Viewpoints of Southern Reconstruction." *Journal of Southern History* 5 (February 1939):49–61.

Singleton, Theresa Ann. "The Archeology of Afro-American Slavery in Coastal Georgia: A Regional Perception of Slave Household and Community Patterns." Ph.D. dissertation, University of Florida, 1980.

Smith, Albert Colbey, "Down Freedom's Road: The Contours of Race, Class, and Property Crime in Black-Belt Georgia, 1866–1910." Ph.D. dissertation, University of Georgia, 1982.

Smith, Allen Candler. "The Republican Party in Georgia, 1867–1871." M.A. thesis, Duke University, 1937.

Spivak, John L. *Georgia Nigger*. New York: Brewer, Warren, and Putnam, 1932.

Stampp, Kenneth M. *The Era of Reconstruction, 1865–1877*. New York: Alfred A. Knopf, 1965.

Stampp, Kenneth M., and Litwack, Leon F., eds. *Reconstruction: An Anthology of Revisionist Writings*. Baton Rouge: Louisiana State University Press, 1969.

Swint, Henry Lee. *The Northern Teacher in the South, 1862–1870*. New York: Octagon Books, 1967.

Taylor, Arnold H. *Travail and Triumph: Black Life and Culture in the South since the Civil War*. Contributions in Afro-American and African Studies, no. 26. Westport, Conn.: Greenwood Press, 1976.

Tebeau, Charlton W. "The Planter in the Lower South, 1865–1880." Ph.D. dissertation, University of Iowa, 1933.

————. "Some Aspects of Planter-Freedmen Relations, 1865–1880." *Journal of Negro History* 21 (April 1936):130–50.

Thomas, David Hurst, et al. *The Anthropology of St. Catherines*

Island: Natural and Cultural History. Vol. 55, part 2. An-
thropological Papers of the American Museum of Natural History. New York: American Museum of Natural History, 1978.

Thomas, Emory M. *The American War and Peace, 1860–1877.* Englewood Cliffs, N.J.: Prentice-Hall, 1973.

————. "The South and the Sea: Some Thoughts on the Southern
Maritime Tradition." *Georgia Historical Quarterly* 67 (Summer
1983):159–67.

Thompson, C. Mildred. "The Freedmen's Bureau in Georgia in
1865–6: An Instrument of Reconstruction." *Georgia Historical
Quarterly* 5 (March 1921):40–49.

————. *Reconstruction in Georgia: Economic, Social, Political,
1865–1872.* 1915. Reprint. Savannah: Beehive Press, 1972.

Toll, William. "Free Men, Freedmen, and Race: Black Social Theory
in the Gilded Age." *Journal of Southern History* 44 (November
1978):571–96.

Van Deburg, William L. *Slavery and Race in American Popular
Culture.* Madison: University of Wisconsin Press, 1984.

Washington, Booker T., and DuBois, W.E.B. *The Negro in the
South: His Economic Progress in Relation to His Moral and Religious Development.* Philadelphia: George W. Jacobs, 1907.

Wiener, Jonathon M. "Class Structure and Economic Development
in the American South, 1865–1955." *American Historical Review*
84 (October 1979):970–1006.

————. *Social Origins of the New South, 1860–1885.* Baton Rouge:
Louisiana State University Press, 1978.

Williamson, Joel. *After Slavery: The Negro in South Carolina during Reconstruction, 1861–1877.* Chapel Hill: University of North
Carolina Press, 1965.

————. *The Crucible of Race: Black-White Relations in the American South since Emancipation.* New York: Oxford University
Press, 1984.

Wingo, Horace C. "Race Relations in Georgia: 1872–1908." Ph.D.
dissertation, University of Georgia, 1969.

Wood, Forrest G. *Black Scare: The Racist Response to Emancipation and Reconstruction.* Berkeley and Los Angeles: University
of California Press, 1968.

Woodman, Harold D. "Sequel to Slavery: The New History Views the Postbellum South." *Journal of Southern History* 43 (November 1977):523–54.

Woodward, C. Vann. *Origins of the New South, 1877–1913*. Baton Rouge: Louisiana State University Press, 1951.

Wooley, Edwin C. *The Reconstruction of Georgia*. New York: Columbia University Press, 1901.

Wylly, Charles Spalding. *The Seed That Was Sown in the Colony of Georgia: The Harvest and the Aftermath, 1740–1870*. New York: Neale, 1910.

Wynes, Charles E. "The Politics of Reconstruction, Redemption, and Bourbonism." In Kenneth Coleman, ed., *A History of Georgia*. pp. 207–24. Athens: University of Georgia Press, 1977.

―――. ed. *The Negro in the South since 1865: Selected Essays in American Negro History*. University, Ala.: University of Alabama Press, 1965.

Wynne, Lewis N. "Planter Politics in Georgia, 1860–1890." Ph.D. dissertation, University of Georgia, 1980.

―――. "The Role of the Freedmen in the Post-Bellum Cotton Economy of Georgia." *Phylon* 42 (December 1981):312–45.

Young, Edward Barham. "The Negro in Georgia Politics, 1867–1877." M.S. thesis, Emory University, 1955.

Zeichner, Oscar. "The Transition from Slave to Free Agricultural Labor in the Southern States." *Agricultural History* 13 (January 1939):22–32.

INDEX